1001 WALKING TIPS

1001 WALKING TIPS

NAVIGATION, FITNESS, GEAR AND SAFETY ADVICE FOR HILLWALKERS, TREKKERS AND URBAN ADVENTURERS

paul besley

Vertebrate Publishing, Sheffield
www.v-publishing.co.uk

First published in 2022 by Vertebrate Publishing.

Vertebrate Publishing
Omega Court, 352 Cemetery Road, Sheffield S11 8FT, United Kingdom.
www.v-publishing.co.uk

A CIP catalogue record for this book is available from the British Library.

ISBN 978-1-83981-076-3 (Paperback)
ISBN 978-1-83981-077-0 (Ebook)

Front cover illustration © Julia Allum represented by www.meiklejohn.co.uk
Photography by Paul Besley unless otherwise credited.

Design by Nathan Ryder, production by Jane Beagley and Cameron Bonser, Vertebrate Publishing.

Printed and bound in Europe by Latitude Press.

Vertebrate Publishing is committed to printing on paper from sustainable sources.

contents

introduction

It ain't what you don't know that gets you into trouble.
It's what you know for sure that just ain't so.
– Mark Twain (attributed)

I hope you picked this book up because you have started walking. I'm meaning the kind of walking that you long for after a heavy week at work. The kind of walking where you can let go of 1,001 things of little consequence and immerse yourself in a landscape of significance.

This book is for the beginner and for those who want to extend their walking to horizons further away. It is designed to help you move from the garden to the mountaintop. It begins at your front door with those first steps of leisurely walking. In recent years, walking has moved down from the hills and mountains and into our own local countryside and urban landscape. Exploring our own immediate environment is a good place to start walking, as there is no need for transport or specialist equipment. What the walker gets is a new outlook on their own terrain, and the stirrings of greater adventures.

To move from the local and urban to the countryside and high places requires a developing skill set. Walking in this new landscape requires no specialist skills; everything is attainable for any individual if you have the capacity to learn and be taught. Some learning is best done with others. Navigation skills and using a map and compass are key skills for the outdoors, and there are plenty of resources and educators who can help anyone develop and improve the use of these basic tools. A skill set for the hill – call it hillcraft – encompasses every aspect of being outdoors, and more often than not being outside on the hill is where we learn. For instance, what to wear is often best learnt on the job. What works for one person does not necessarily work for another. In fact, the expertise of appraising and making up your own mind is one of the best skills to learn. The 1,001 walking tips in this book come from my own personal experience. Some I have learnt on courses, many were taught by more experienced walkers, and the majority are from my own knowledge of almost 50 years on the hill.

Walking is a superb way of keeping fit. It is a low-cost activity that gives a high return for a lifetime. I had two aims when I set out to write this book. The first was to show the beginner and aspiring master the way forward to having a lifetime of days out walking. The second was to underline that the goal of walking is to return home safely. The summit will always be there another day. If the book achieves those two aims, it will have been a success.

Happy safe walking!

Scout, the perfect walking companion.

Cloud inversion at North Lees Hall in the Peak District.

acknowledgements

My thanks go to the team at Vertebrate Publishing, especially Jon Barton, John Coefield, Kirsty Reade and Emma Lockley. To the people of Twitter who shared their top tips. To Tomo Thompson, who shared with me 'A pound in the pocket is lighter than a pound on the back' as he handed me his rucksack (heavy) to carry (*tip 978*). To Sarah Turner for the £10 note (*tip 9*).To Alison Counsell for all the cooked meals outdoors (*tip 939*). To Scout for all the walks and never ever once sharing food (*tip 983*) but costing me a fortune in unwanted food (*tip 985*). To the dozens of specialists in independent outdoor shops who spend time and share their experience with customers, a task that is occasionally thankless, but more often than not rewarding (*tip 718*). To the volunteers who clear the paths, pick the litter, save the distressed, tell the stories and show the way to the future, thank you for all you do (*tips 986–991*). To the public who stop and chat and pat a dog and share their day, that is what it is all about.

feedback and updates

Nothing stays the same.

When I began walking, we just had a map and a compass and no thought (other than in sci-fi films) of GPS, smartphones, breathable clothing or social media. I took half a dozen pictures because film was expensive and even more costly to get processed; now I take 400–500 photos on every walk with my digital camera and, yes, most are still rubbish.

If something does change, or you have a different and constructive perspective on any of the points, then drop me a note at 1001walkingtips@gmail.com

If you have an overwhelming desire to throw out some negativity go to TL 32708 23552.

Looking out from Wilderness Gully to Dove Stone Reservoir.

Immerse yourself in a landscape. © *walkhighlands*

001

BASICS (1–105)

'There comes a time on every walk where it all makes perfect sense and there is no place you would rather be and nothing you would rather be doing.'

Switch on your outdoor muscles and switch off from the stresses of daily life.

BASICS (1-105)

THE GOLDEN RULES (1-5)

1. Always tell someone where you are going. Not the person with you, but someone at home, a friend, your mum, the YHA manager. Tell them when you expect to be back, and what to do if you aren't. Write it down. Write your phone number down too.

2. Plan and prepare. Where to go. How to get there. What to do if things go wrong.

3. Always have a map and compass and know how to use them. Have the skills and experience to go where you want to go. Have enough food and drink for the whole day and a little bit more.

4. Wear appropriate clothing for the terrain and weather conditions. Happy feet begin with good quality socks and footwear. Don't forget the waterproofs.

5. Treat the landscape with respect, as though you are a guest. Take a phone but switch it off. Save the battery and enjoy the peace. Have fun. Be happy.

THINGS TO REMEMBER (6-28)

6. At the start of a walk, switch on the outdoor muscles in body and mind. Leave the hometown muscles just inside your front door.

7. If with others, talk about the day, what you will see, how long you will walk before stopping, when and where you will have lunch. Take out a map and look at the landscape around you before you set off from the rendezvous point. Use this time to engage your mind and body. Tick off the things you need to be prepared for: rough terrain, water, steep ascent or descent, exposure. Develop a mental storyboard of what you will see and encounter on the route.

8. When setting out on a walk, keep personal items such as car keys in a safe place where they won't be disturbed throughout the day. A good place to keep car keys is in the inner pocket of the rucksack lid, where there should be a clip to safely attach them to. Don't open this pocket again until you get back to the car.

9. A £10 note slipped into the back of a phone case or deep inside a pack can be a gift in an emergency. Always keep a tenner as a backup.

10. Don't forget midge cream. Especially in Scotland.

11. Keep hydrated during the walk. This is perhaps the number one piece of safety advice. Staying hydrated can stop the mind from becoming confused and the body from breaking down, and allows the post-walk restorative process within our bodies to be more effective.

12. Stop regularly for a snack and a drink. Intervals can be a personal thing, but planning a break every one or two hours in your day will help sustain your walking and make it much more enjoyable.

13. Put snacks in a pocket that is easy to access to allow you to graze on them without having to remove your pack.

14. If you find you need to keep taking your pack off to get at items, really consider where those items should be stored. And whether those items should be carried at all.

15. Be mindful of mixed-use trails with bikes and horses. Try to mostly stay on the left and don't wander all over the trail. Keep aware of what is behind you. And be nice. Say hello. Smile. It's good for you!

16. Fit a falconry bell to your dog's collar so that you can always hear where they are.

BASICS (1–105)

17. Learn to walk at your natural pace. I learnt this lesson when on my first long-distance walk. After a few days, I realised that I had a natural pace and that if I kept to it, I could walk more easily for longer and not tire myself out.

18. Keep a pace that enables you to hold a normal conversation with people, even if going uphill – breathing acts as a natural metronome to our efforts. If walking in a group, the pace should be that of the slowest person.

19. If faster people leave others behind, all that happens is the faster group has to wait. And probably won't get invited on the next walk.

20. Unless you are on a challenge walk, or need to get somewhere for public transport, it isn't a race. Stop and enjoy the views.

21. Never walk with your laces undone. This is a recipe for disaster.

22. When walking downhill, keep the centre of gravity over your feet. Don't lean, as this can cause you to slip and fall backwards, or stumble forwards.

23. You are generally more susceptible to injury coming down than going up. It is very rare for someone to fall going up a hill, but common for people to stumble and trip going down a hill. Take your time; rest if necessary.

24. Most slips and trips happen towards the end of the walk when people are relaxing and looking forward to the pub or getting home. They stop paying attention to what their feet are doing. Never walk while looking at your phone. This is another recipe for disaster.

25. If you stumble, stop. Stand up straight and take a minute to let your body and mind reset. Trying to recover by rushing on will only end in another stumble.

26. Look back occasionally. The view will be different and will quite often be a surprise.

27. The best kind of walking is where you walk into the landscape, allowing the space to envelop you, helping you to become part of the environment. As this happens, you usually become silent as the nature of your position reveals itself to you.

28. There comes a time on every walk where it all makes perfect sense and there is no place you would rather be and nothing you would rather be doing. This is the golden time. And it is an emotional place. Nothing else matters at that moment. This is what walking is all about.

WEATHER (29–48)

29. Walk in all weathers. A rain-sodden walk can be miserable, it's true, but if you are used to it – and in the UK, who isn't? – you can develop your clothing and gear system to enable you to cope with it in relative comfort. Walking in heat requires more fluids, protection and a slower pace. Learn to spot signs that you need to stop or change something about you or the walk.

30. Cold and rain affect our mood drastically when outdoors. This is something worth getting used to, and there is plenty of opportunity in the UK. Walk in poor weather, even if it is just around the local streets. Do it for a long period, a few hours, and note how your mood changes. Then work out what you need to do to keep the mood positive and upbeat.

31. Walking on a dry summer day is very different from walking in a winter storm across a featureless moorland. Both can be just as rewarding, but one needs a different mindset from the other. The only way to train your mind to accept both types of experience is to immerse yourself in those environments.

32. Walk into the hills cold by wearing fewer layers than you have with you. That way you won't sweat and get clammy and uncomfortable, and stink, and spend the rest of the walk trying to dry out your skin and clothing.

33. Vent regularly. Let the heat escape, even in winter, before it turns into moisture and you begin to cool too rapidly.

34. Hyperthermia can kill. Learn how to deal with it should someone begin to overheat. Cooling and shade are a must to start the process of bringing the temperature down.

35. Hypothermia can also kill. In cold and especially wet weather, make sure no one is suffering. The symptoms include shivering, cold, slurred speech and confusion. It can come on quickly and in the most benign of situations. I once had a walking companion suffer from early onset hypothermia as we walked up the Cut Gate bridleway in the Peak District on a fairly calm and reasonably warm day.

36. When you stop in cold weather, try to find somewhere out of the wind. If ascending to a mountain summit, stop before you reach the top to keep out of the cold, driving wind. As soon as you stop, put on another layer or switch to an insulation jacket and air the one you have been wearing, then switch back when you begin walking again.

37. A small umbrella can be useful for those intermittent showers that last a few minutes. It saves you taking your pack off and donning waterproofs, only to have the rain stop shortly afterwards. Remember to dry out the brolly when the rain stops, and don't use an umbrella in high winds. It won't work.

38. If you wear spectacles and you have driving rain running straight into your face, that will affect visibility. But it will also affect your mindset, which can have serious consequences should you have to endure these conditions for an extended period in a more remote area. Assess what is happening and collect it as data. Develop new strategies to deal with the conditions so you are comfortable in the environment. For instance, wear contact lenses, or a peaked cap under your hood to deal with rain.

39. I used to wear contact lenses because I got sick of not being able to see in wet weather, until one day when winter walking on a Scottish mountain the wind blew one lens out, leaving me with only one good eye, which I thought at the time was a real problem. I started to tentatively walk off the hill with the party I was with, but I realised I could see the map clearly without my reading glasses, and I could also see the landscape clearly. What had happened was my brain had done the maths and worked out that by combining both images, depending on the distance I was focusing at, I could have crystal-clear vision. Apparently, this is well known to mountaineers, but was a revelation to me.

40. Testing out your gear will pay dividends. Pay attention to leaks, body warmth, ease of use and cooling effect in heat.

41. Sunblock is a must, at least factor 50. The wind that is blowing cooling air across the moor won't protect you from sunburn, which can be severe.

42. In the UK the prevailing wind is from the west. On windy days, walking into the wind may impede progress and cause vision to be lost as the eyes stream. It may be useful to have protective eyewear to keep the eyes clear.

43. Always keep an eye on the time and the weather.

44. Take note of where the sun is in relation to the horizon to give you a sense of when the day will be closing in.

45. What happens if you don't make it off the hill in time? Try it one night in safety, having first let someone know where you are and that you are OK. Stay out, gauge how it feels, see what you need to have with you to make it a less inhospitable experience. Then make any changes and repeat until you have a way of surviving in relative comfort and safety.

46. Learn how your gear functions. If it is going to hammer it down with rain, pack waterproofs. Or maybe don't, if you want to find out how not having waterproofs affects your mind and body. Does having a peaked baseball cap help visibility? Do over-trousers stay up when they are sodden? Does that cold trickle down the back mean you have a leaky jacket or do you need to pay more attention to how you use the item?

47. Identify what gear works for you and stick to it. Don't become a hostage to each new fad or gadget that comes along. And we all do.

48. If you want to prepare yourself for the Pennine Way and know that at some point you may well get bad weather, really bad weather, it's a good idea to begin conditioning your mind, body and gear to it. Watch the weather forecast and when you spot some bad weather, plan a walk along a route that is well known to you. Think about the effects the weather will have on you, and try to develop strategies for dealing with it before you set off.

WATER (49–58)

49. After periods of heavy rain, rivers and streams will be running high and with force, so plan to avoid crossing these without a bridge when looking at a route.

50. Never cross raging water by foot. Always use a bridge or find an alternative route.

51. When crossing streams and rivers, undo the buckles on your pack, so that should you stumble and fall you can release the pack to stop it tipping you over to drown.

52. Always use walking poles when crossing a river. Make sure you have three points of contact before moving position. Choose a crossing point where the water is not raging and look for a calm pool, even if it means getting more of your leg wet.

53. Try to keep boots dry when crossing a wide, deep river by taking them off and tying the laces around your neck so that they hang over your shoulder. Roll your trousers up, take your socks off, step firmly in bare feet into the water and slowly work your way across. At the other end, dry your feet on a towel and put your socks and boots back on.

54. Whenever rivers and streams are low and you have the choice between a bridge or a ford to cross them, choose the ford. It's much more fun.

Stepping stones at Chee Dale in the Peak District.

55. Take care when using stepping stones after high water levels, as they can be slippery.

56. When there is a line of people waiting to use stepping stones, and water levels are low, just walk through the water. It makes you look hard and very experienced. Even if the water is flooding your boots. (Wear gaiters.)

57. Don't enter water in a Site of Special Scientific Interest (SSSI). It may be that some rare species, for instance the English native crayfish, is living there.

58. When walking along a river, look out for dippers, water voles and dragonflies.

FEET (59–65)

59. Foot placement is just as important when walking as it is in climbing. Get used to feeling how your foot feels when it is on firm ground. When moving over boulder fields, slopes or scree, a firmer boot will give more stability than one that is flexible.

60. Rub feet and other bits in a small amount of Vaseline to prevent chafing.

61. If you feel a hotspot on your feet while walking, stop immediately and check what is going on. The start of a blister can be alleviated by adjusting lacing or applying blister plasters.

62. If you have a long descent, adjust your lacing so your foot doesn't keep sliding forward in your footwear and ramming your toes against the end of the toe box.

63. When you stop in warm weather, take off your boots and air those feet and socks.

64. Sticking your feet in a cold stream at the end of a day is a great way to revitalise tired feet.

65. If your toenails are bruised and blackened at the end of a day's walking, trim your nails or get boots that fit your feet, or both.

FITNESS AND TRAINING (66–105)

66. Walking is our first great achievement. The one where we did it. Those first few toddler steps open a vast new world of discovery and connection. We continue the journey for many years, until we get our first car and then the connection begins to stretch, and we start to lose the feel of the land-scape. Our journeys become about time and speed and metal and plastic, and how we think others perceive us because of what we drive and where we live and work. Getting back to walking reconnects us with the adventure of life.

Practise your balance by moving over uneven terrain.

67. Walking is good for health and the planet. It is low-cost and sustainable, needs no special equipment to begin, can be done anywhere and at any time, and has low impact on the environment.

68. If you are just taking up walking as an activity, be realistic about your fitness levels. It is a simple equation: the fitter you are, the more you will get out of walking. Work on fitness daily. A simple morning routine of stretches can free muscles and bones from their night-time strictures.

69. If you are new to walking, take things easy at first. A walk around the block can be an enjoyable experience, especially in summer, when the gardens are full of flowers and people are out and about wanting to talk and socialise.

70. Have a walking friend, someone who you can meet up with, go for a walk with, have a coffee and a chat with. The mental health benefits of something as simple as this are beyond estimation.

71. When heading out into the countryside for your first walk, choose one that is popular, has interesting features and is near to any transport connections. A walk across challenging Rannoch Moor is probably not the one to choose.

72. Skill fade is an issue after being away from the outdoors for any period. As you move back into the hills, begin slowly in a safe environment to prevent any serious incidents.

73. Learn how to walk. Weight over the centre of gravity, just below the sternum, posture upright, balance evenly distributed. Posture is important. Being bent over, folding under the weight of a heavy pack, will restrict movement and breathing. Walking upright helps the body get more oxygen and takes strain away from the back and legs.

74. Limber up before a walk. Warming the muscles and bits of stretchy tissue makes walking more comfortable and helps prevent injury. Have a basic warm-up routine, doing stretching exercises, loosening those joints, relaxing those shoulders.

75. Strength and flexibility are the key to a good physical walk. The demands placed on a human body differ greatly depending on the terrain you are going to cover; a basic level of fitness is a good foundation.

76. The more we exercise, the stronger the nerve connections become. These help to fire groups of muscles when we need them on the hill, keeping us safe as we move through a landscape.

77. A 'couch to 5K' programme is a great way to build up mileage, stamina and strength.

78. Running is good for stamina. Going uphill with a pack on requires more than strength – it needs a good cardio system. Running can give you this.

79. Balance is important when moving over uneven terrain. One way to assess how good you are at balancing your body is to walk over rough terrain while going up a steep slope – a scramble section, a rocky slope below an escarpment, or a decent boulder field with not too many leg-breakers. Practise moving up and down the area with your arms folded across your chest. This brings your core into play a lot more and will reveal just how in balance you are.

80. Balancing on one foot really helps me to see how well my core is doing. Raising a knee while doing it intensifies the sense of lack of balance. Obviously, I don't do this on a knife-edge ridge or at the top of the stairs.

BASICS (1-105)

81. Slacklining is a great way to build balance and core strength. Try it out in the garden and see how it improves your ability to move more easily over difficult ground.

82. Once you are moving, you want to keep moving. Develop your fitness, skills and equipment to ensure you don't have to keep stopping.

83. Formulate a simple exercise regime for everyday use that concentrates on keeping the limbs supple and free from any mechanical restriction in movement. Leg raises, exercises of the torso, arm and shoulder exercises, and rotational exercises all help with keeping the body elastic.

84. Working on core strength is one of the keys to allowing you to move through more exhilarating terrain and keeping the body from becoming tired too soon. The glutes, the big curve of your bum, are where the power should come from for walking. This makes it easier on the rest of the body. Choose some exercises that fire these up. You can feel the effect almost immediately as you start walking from the glutes and not the lower back. Work on your lower back and hips. Try to get as much movement into these as possible.

85. For free workouts to help you exercise safely, watch the Fitness Studio videos on the NHS website (***www.nhs.uk/conditions/nhs-fitness-studio***).

86. Having a good aerobic system will help enormously for those big hill days. If you are setting out to walk where there will be lots of ascent and descent, train for it. Find a steep hill, one where you might have to use a hand occasionally. Fill your pack with water bottles and do hill reps. Start by walking up at your normal pace. Don't stop but keep going, even if it hurts. Time yourself, then repeat a few times. By taking the average time, you will get a baseline. Gradually add weight as you begin to beat your baseline. Keep a record of your times and use this log to assess your aerobic fitness.

87. If you need a serious improvement in fitness, think about teaming up with an instructor or a group.

88. Use a heart-rate monitor to track your progress. Knowing your resting heart rate (RHR) and maximum heart rate (MHR), you can set training and recovery heart rate targets.

89. Keep a logbook of walks and training to show progression. Make notes on what worked, how you felt and what you might change.

90. Mental resilience and a pragmatic approach are probably the greatest and strongest assets to have. You can only build resilience by doing it, by being in the storm. There is no other way.

91. The ability to bounce back from some adversity, like going the wrong way or getting caught in bad weather, can make a big difference to a day out.

92. Once you have the basic skills of navigation firmly in your mind and hands, the rest is about how you train your mind and body to deal with new landscapes and environments. Learning how to navigate a featureless landscape in a winter storm can only be taught by doing that. But it would be foolish to make that the starting point of a walking career. You need to build up to it.

93. Conditioning requires a slow, methodical process of engagement with a given environment – hot or cold, wet or dry. It is about working out what is happening to the body and mind, and developing strategies and mechanisms that allow you to fully function in those conditions. This takes time and practice.

Squeeze stiles can add time to a walk.

Train by walking through different types of terrain.

BASICS (1–105)

94. Once you begin, conditioning acts like building blocks for the next step up in your walking career, shortening the learning process because you are using empirical experience and knowledge to take you further.

95. Spend lots of time walking the same type of terrain before moving on to more difficult walking. This gets you used to the landscape and how to move in it, and helps tone your body.

96. Include small sections of new terrain in existing walks. Add a section of off-path walking across a moor to a lowland walk, so that your mind and body can feel the transition.

97. The trick in training for walking is not to push it so far that you sustain injuries and have to stop. Methodical and gradual is the way.

98. Train for long walks by building up slowly. Extend the distance covered over a period of time. Add weight gradually, but not at the same time as distance.

99. Train for multi-day walks in the mountains by gradually extending walks from one day to two, and then three, etc. And make sure you get in plenty of ascent and descent. Don't train for the Tour du Mont Blanc by walking through the farmlands of Lincolnshire.

100. Train your body for the landscape you are walking through. A day of lowland walking makes very different stresses on the lower back than a winter's day walking in the mountains of Scotland. Have walks that are used for training purposes.

101. The point of a training walk is research. You are collecting valuable data to give you a baseline of behaviour for given conditions and environment. When out on the walk, think about what is happening to you and to your gear, what is performing well, what is failing, and how your mind and body are coping.

102. When planning out a route, work forwards and backwards. Make a note of what you should be able to see at different stages and keep your horizon shifting from that which is far away to that which is near. In poor visibility, knowing what you should be encountering close by is a good navigation tool.

103. Walk at night. Oddly, this can be safer in the wilderness than in a city urban environment. Night-time walking requires different skills and gives a different experience. A walk with a full moon can mean you dispense with a head torch. A walk on a cloudy night means visibility can be just the few metres around you. Your body will also be subjected to the change in the environmental conditions, the night air cooling, condensation forming. Wildlife may well be more abundant as nocturnal animals and birds venture forth. Being surprised by a badger on the path or an owl silently passing over your head is a wonderful experience.

104. A walk really does begin with a single step, and it continues that way too. Break walks down into small chunks. A walk of 1,000 miles is difficult to hold in the mind. So are ten 100-mile walks. But ten days of 10 miles each day is something we can all relate to. Make the walk relatable.

105. Being able to move easily through any landscape helps us explore new places, travel further and quicker, and remain alert to those special moments.

Look for public rights of way.

ERMAID
ORRIDGE
PUBLIC FOOTPATH
PUBLIC FOOTPATH

Identify features like a stream junction or ford.

NAVIGATION (106–208)

'Never map-read and walk at the same time. That cliff edge you are looking at on the ma—'

NAVIGATION (106–208)

BASICS (106–113)

106. If someone says they don't need a map to go on a walk, be wary.

107. If you know where you are, you can't be lost. Always keep a track of your present location.

108. The two main aspects of successful navigation are direction and distance. Knowing how to use these will mean you have less trouble.

109. Learn navigation using a map and a compass. This is a basic skill. Until you have mastered using these two pieces of equipment, stay away from phone-based apps or GPS devices.

110. Book on to the National Navigation Award Scheme (***www.nnas.org.uk***). This scheme has three levels – bronze, silver and gold – and is a non-competitive way of learning navigational skills for use in the outdoors.

111. If you want to lead groups in upland, moorland and mountain walking areas, or just want to have better skills in these environments, book on to a Mountain Training scheme (***www.mountain-training.org***). These cover walking in lowland areas and progress to hill, mountain and even international mountain leader schemes.

112. Once you have mastered summer walking and want to move on to winter walking in the high mountains, look at the Winter Mountain Leader scheme at Mountain Training.

113. If you find a footpath blocked, or with a damaged stile or gate, you can report it to your local council. Doing this helps preserve the footpath network for everyone, now and in the future. Every council will have online, definitive maps showing where every legal Public Right of Way is. Each PRoW has a number that you can refer to in any correspondence.

MAP AND COMPASS (114–166)

114. Ordnance Survey maps are the most widely used in Britain, and cover all the land. The maps are very rarely wrong. Use the 1:50,000 maps for a general view and planning, and for high mountain walking. Use the greater detail in the 1:25,000 maps for lowland and upland walking.

115. Each OS map has a number. OL maps are produced for the national parks and the more popular areas.

116. OL1 is the 1:25,000 map for the Dark Peak area of the Peak District. To buy the standard OS maps that cover the area featured in OL1, you would need to get 268, 277, 278 and 288. It makes sense to have just one map.

117. Learn the map legends, which are on the side of all OS maps. Be able to differentiate a Public Right of Way footpath (on the 1:25,000 map a green dashed line, meaning anyone can walk along the path) from a concession path (a black dashed line, meaning not a PRoW and open under the discretion of the landowner), a bridleway (a thick green line with long dashes, meaning walkers, horses and bicycles have a PRoW along the generally wide-ish track) and a byway open to all traffic (a thick green line with dashes and crenellations, meaning walkers, horses, cycles, cars and motorbikes all have a PRoW).

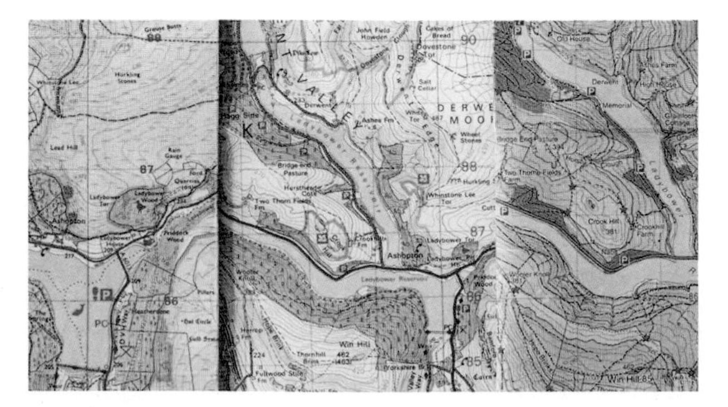

Familiarise yourself with different map scales.

Compare features on the map to the landscape around you to build navigation skills.

Keep checking where you are.

NAVIGATION (106–208)

118. Learn to use different scale maps, like 1:25,000, 1:40,000 and 1:50,000. Take note of how the different maps make you interact with the landscape. 1:25,000 is great for detail; 1:50,000 gives a superb overview; 1:40,000 looks and feels very different. The most ubiquitous 1:40,000 maps are the Harvey British Mountain Maps. These are essentially contour maps, with the contours shown in bands of colour as the height increases. Walls and boundaries have been removed so that the navigator has a clear view of the landscape, its shape and relationship. For an experienced navigator, this makes crossing such terrain much simpler and quicker.

119. Ordnance Survey grid references convert longitude and latitude to a simple numerical system that covers the country. Longitude begins at the Greenwich Observatory and moves east around the world. Each Ordnance Survey map starts in the south-west corner. Grid references give the sheet name (two letters), followed by two sets of three, four or five numbers (the more figures, the more specific the area, effectively zooming in on a location). The first of these sets gives the easterly reference or 'easting' (going left to right across the map), and the second gives the northerly reference or 'northing' (going bottom to top on the map). You can remember the order by saying 'go along the corridor (easting) and up the stairs (northing)'.

120. Let's take the grid reference TQ 38883 77315 as an example. The letters TQ take you to a 100-kilometre square in south-east England. The first number in each set splits this big area into 10-kilometre squares, with the gridlines numbered from 0 to 9, so TQ 3 7 narrows this down to somewhere in Greenwich. London. TQ 38 77 puts you in a garden in Ashburnham Grove, London SE10. Adding an extra number to give you TQ 388 773 puts you in the south-west corner of a 100-metre square in Greenwich Park. And TQ 3888 7731 puts you at the corner of a 10-metre square by Greenwich Observatory. Finally, TQ 38883 77315 puts you in a one-metre square standing directly above the prime meridian at Greenwich Observatory. See, it's simple!

121. The horizontal and vertical thin blue lines are not superbly constructed straight canals – they are the grid squares that navigators use to see where they are. For example, on 1:25,000 maps the gridlines have a number written in large blue figures every kilometre going east and north.

122. Each square covers one kilometre, whether it is on a 1:25,000 map or a 1:50,000 scale map. Whoa, how can that be? (This is evidence of the dark arts practised by the cartographers at OS.)

123. OS maps are coloured, as are Harvey maps – quite beautifully, in fact. Green for woodlands; white for land; beige for access land; black lines for boundary walls or fences, or railways; blue for streams and bodies of water; blue, red, yellow or brown for roads. Grey lines for crags and mountains; brown lines for contours. This gives a quick and easy overview of the terrain.

124. Remove the map cover to make it easier to fold the map to just where you need it, reflecting the ground that you are on and moving towards. Save the cover to store with the map when not in use.

125. Laminated maps last much longer than plain paper maps and are worth the extra investment. You can also write on a laminated map and then wipe it clean after use.

126. Use strong rubber bands to keep laminated maps folded on the correct grid points.

127. If you can only get standard paper maps, use a ziplock bag to protect them from the rain and store them in your map pocket. Map cases around the neck have a habit of getting in the way.

NAVIGATION (106–208)

128. Subscription to the OS website (***www.ordnancesurvey.co.uk***) gives you online mapping on all your devices so you can access your own routes or thousands of others on a smartphone when out on the hill.

129. The Ordnance Survey online mapping service is excellent. You can view an area, a route in a variety of scales, satellite and three-dimensional imagery, cityscapes and green spaces. Spending time searching out images of the terrain can give you valuable information for a long trip.

130. Print routes from the OS online site on to A4 waterproof paper. Don't use a laminating machine. Waterproof paper stops the glare from a head torch reflecting off an office-type lamination plastic and ruining your night vision.

131. If you are on a multi-day walk, using printed maps from the OS website can save you a huge amount in weight and bulk from not having to carry multiple or bigger maps.

132. Day walks are good for practising micronavigation. Choose a nearby feature on a walk. Follow a stream to where it forks, measure the distance and calculate how much time and distance it should take you to get there. Look for re-entrants, small incisions in the hillside, as these are good navigation features to practise map-reading skills with. Use 'handrails' such as a long wall or side of a woodland to practise 'aiming off': deliberately walking to a bearing to the left or right of the arrival point, then tracking back to it by following the handrail. This saves you missing the location, which can happen if you are aiming straight at it, particularly in bad weather.

133. Using a map while out walking is one of the basic skills that is easily transferred into any terrain. But never map-read and walk at the same time. That cliff edge you are looking at on the ma—

134. The best way to use an map for navigation is by looking at the contours to see what the land is doing. Harvey maps are particularly good for this. The closer the contours are to each other, the steeper the terrain. Some maps have contours every ten metres, but some have them every five metres – check the map legend and the numbers on the contour lines.

135. Look at the land and the map and match the contour lines on the map with the land to gain a better understanding of the terrain.

136. Winter is really good for learning to navigate solely by contours. In heavy snowfall, paths and boundaries can be obliterated, leaving a white landscape of slopes and plains.

137. Slope aspect, the direction a slope faces, is one of the most useful navigation tools you have. It is an infallible way of getting the direction.

138. Valleys are also useful to establish location. A map showing a valley that has tightly packed contours in a 'V' shape and a river at the bottom is a narrow steep-sided gorge. A valley that has steep sides and a wide bottom can be a dry valley as the land has been created by glacial movement. Learn to tell the difference between the two.

139. Spot heights are small orange, black or blue dots on maps that show the height of the land at that point. They are good for setting the altimeter on watches and positioning devices.

You can use a resection to triangulate your position on a map.

140. Learning to use an altimeter can help when navigating complicated ground. Using the height and the contours marked on the map can give you a vertical position that you can then use to locate yourself in the landscape.

141. Look on the map for a small blue triangle with a blue dot in the centre. This is an Ordnance Survey triangulation pillar and children of all ages love ticking these off. There are over 6,500 in the UK.

142. Learn how to do a resection. This skill is vital for locating your position in a landscape with lots of similar features. From your position, take a bearing, preferably around 60, 180 and 300 degrees, and draw the line on the map. Where they intersect, a small triangle, is your position. This makes you look massively skilled in front of others. But it is an essential skill to have in mountain areas.

143. When practising navigation on day walks, test your accuracy with a GPS device. This will give you valuable information about your skill level and what you need to work on to improve.

144. Learn how long it takes you to walk 100 metres and one kilometre. Then you can estimate how long it will take you to reach the next feature or stop, or the end of the walk. Find a running track and walk around it at your natural pace. Time yourself and divide the time by the distance walked to work out your time per 100 metres.

145. Practise estimating distance in different terrain: a flat featureless moor, a series of rocky crags, a steep mountainside. Get used to knowing how long it will take for you to get to a certain point ahead of you in these terrains.

146. The simplest way to gauge distance on a map is to use the roamer scale on the compass base. For finer measurement, use the ruler scale.

147. From the map, identify a feature a few hundred metres ahead and locate it in the landscape. Looking at the map, study the land that you will be moving over and build up a picture of it in your mind. Then walk to the feature, feel what the landscape is doing and compare that to what you thought it would do.

148. Navigating across a moor full of groughs (deep gullies or fissures, *tip 491*) is a true test of navigation skill, particularly at night. Use visual points to navigate to, keeping each section short and as much in a direct line as possible. (Hint: this is almost impossible to do, but it is a nice thought to put in a book.)

149. Use Naismith's Rule (*tip 516*) to calculate times when entering mountain terrain. Add one minute for every 10 metres of ascent, and one hour for every 5 kilometres walked, to estimate the time taken to walk the distance between two points.

NAVIGATION (106–208)

150. A black boundary line denoting a fence or a wall on a map does not necessarily mean that one exists on the ground. If OS maps show a wall but when you get there nothing can be seen, look for a small rise in the land. Often, wall foundations are still evident beneath the grass and bracken, or the footpath may in fact be the base of the wall.

151. The width of a river or stream can be assessed by the width of the blue line on the map. While not massively accurate, this does give a good representation. If a map shows a river bounded by two bold blue lines, this indicates a significant body of water and one that you are not going to be able to cross on foot, other than via a bridge or a boat – or a swim.

152. Some blue lines are canals, and these make for a relaxing day walk, as they are usually flat and straight, and often have great pubs. But if you have dogs, mind that they do not jump into a lock which is too deep for you to get them out.

153. Maps are not always accurate around forests, as they can get cut down before a new map is produced. Learn to use contours, as they almost never move.

154. In good visibility you should not need to use a compass, as the map should be sufficient.

155. Moving over terrain at night means dividing the journey into shorter legs so that you can navigate quickly between points.

156. Learn navigation techniques like aiming off (*tip 132*), boxing (going around a feature), linear features (boundaries, streams, roads) and slope aspects (which way a slope is facing on the map and on the land). The OS website has loads of information and examples of how you can practise and use these techniques (***https://getoutside.ordnancesurvey.co.uk***).

157. In bad weather, in order to maintain the correct course with a party, use people to leapfrog ahead along the route, sending one person in front but keeping them visible, then moving the party up to them and then repeating until you reach your destination or the visibility improves.

158. Compasses may not work in some mountain ranges like the magnetic Cuillins on Skye. Be aware of this when planning routes and navigating through the terrain.

159. A baseplate compass, such as the Silva Ranger, is the best to use with a map as it allows the compass to sit flat on the map, enabling you to rotate both at the same time to orientate yourself in the landscape.

160. Always use a compass with a baseplate that is marked with roamer scales and a ruler. It should have a rotating bezel marked with 360 degrees, and a red arrow for north. The basic compass has a 1:25,000 scale roamer along with a 1:50,000 scale. 1:40,000 scale roamers are also available for use with Harvey Mountain Maps. They have a four-centimetre ruler marked in one-millimetre increments that is good for measuring fine distances.

161. Practise using a map and compass in a variety of terrains (both known and unknown) and weather conditions.

162. Begin by always orientating the map and compass so that the map is pointing in the same direction as your travel and reflects the ground you are moving over.

163. Place the compass on the map and set them both to north, then adjust the compass to your line of travel on the map, keeping the red arrow pointing north, and take your bearing to the feature you are walking to from your present location on the map.

164. Magnetic variation needs to be allowed for because the compass points to magnetic north and not grid north. The magnetic variation changes over time, so don't forget to add the amount stated on the map to your calculation.

165. When taking a bearing, use your knee to rest the map on so that you can maintain a steady position.

166. Practise using a map and compass in bad weather and low cloud where visibility is down to a few metres. Do this in a wide open space and away from cliff edges. Get used to how it feels and what techniques you need to use.

NATURAL NAVIGATION (167–178)

167. Natural navigation, using the natural world to help you move around, is something that can supplement map and compass.

168. Watersheds are useful to know about in an area. For instance, the streams and rivers in the Peak District ultimately flow into the North Sea or the Irish Sea to the east and west.

169. North/south plays a big part in using the natural world to navigate by. In the northern hemisphere, we get most of our sun from the south. Using this, we can look at plants and trees, whose leaves will gravitate towards the sun, therefore giving most growth on the southern side.

170. Beech trees in English woodland often have an orange growth (Trentepohlia) on the bark. These algae thrive in moist, cool environments and can be found on the north-facing part of the tree trunk.

171. The sun of course moves east to west, which is always good to remember when planning that summit trip to watch the sunrise or sunset.

172. The tips of a crescent moon extrapolated down to the horizon give the general direction of the south in the northern hemisphere, and north in the southern hemisphere.

173. Using the North Star, or the Pole Star as it is also known, can show us where true north is, which is directly below the star.

174. In the UK, the prevailing winds come from somewhere between the west and south-west. This means that any branches of trees or bushes exposed to the wind will point towards the east to north-east.

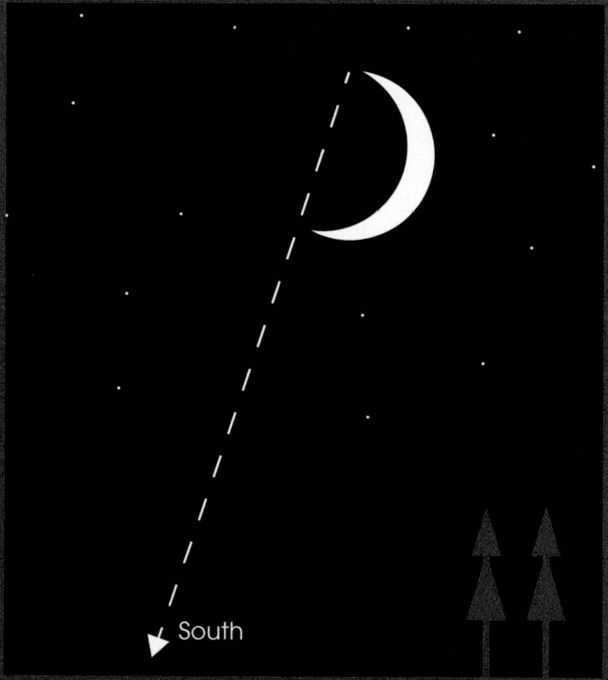

South

Navigation using the moon.

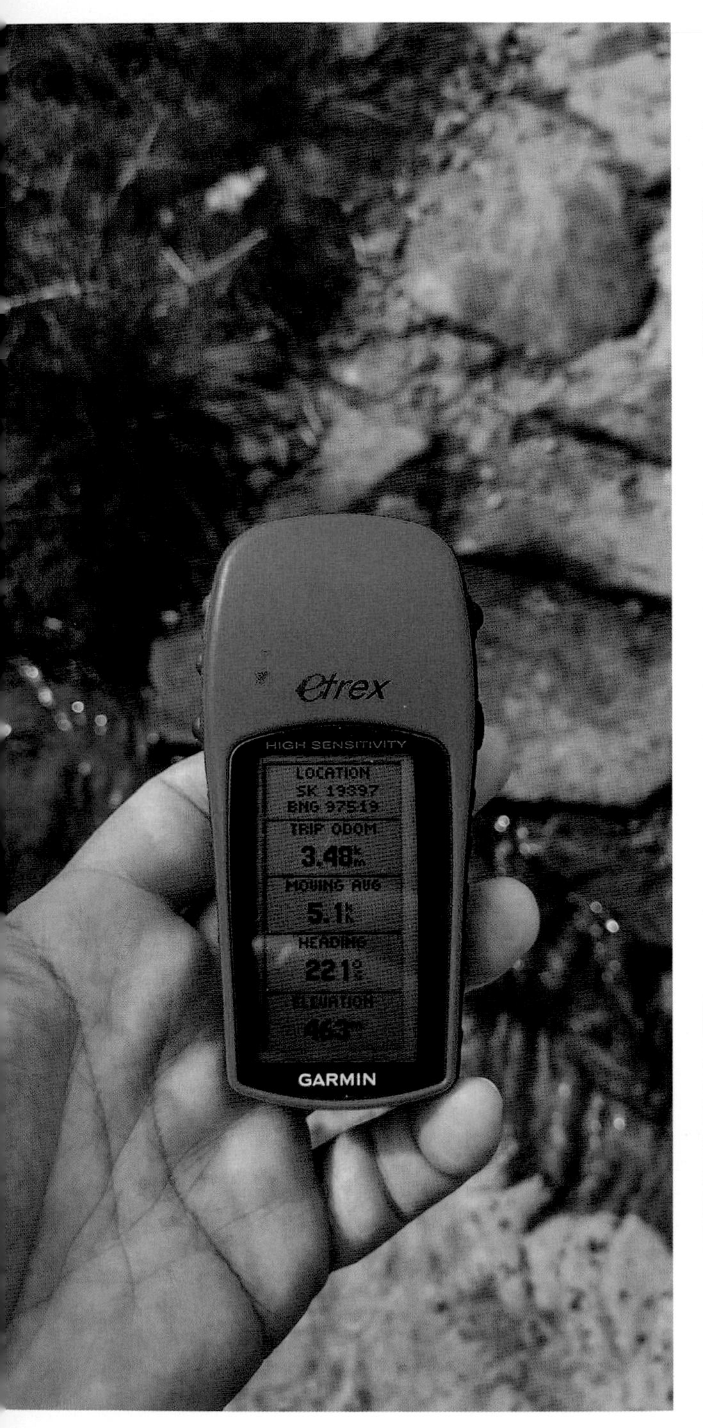

Test your pacing with a GPS check.

175. Water flows downhill, so you can follow a watercourse to get off a hill in poor visibility. Just watch out for any waterfalls tumbling off the edge of a cliff.

176. As water flows towards the valley, the width and depth will increase, so when looking for a crossing point always head uphill.

177. A dry river or stream bed will show bedrock or stone.

178. In limestone country, rivers can disappear in dry months, so look for expanses of stone fringed with tall grasses and riverside plants.

GPS AND DIGITAL DEVICES (179–208)

179. These days, many people use a GPS device for navigation. There is nothing wrong with this as long as a few rules are followed, the main one being to always carry a paper map and compass as backup.

180. Most people now seem to own a GPS device. I have several, including ones on old phones now languishing in the backs of drawers. We should learn how they work and how to use them.

181. GPS devices use Global Positioning Systems to determine your location via satellites. By triangulating your device, the GPS can then give you an accurate fix on your location. To do this it needs three things: to have power, to have a clear line of sight of the sky, and to be switched on.

182. You can get GPS on standalone units like the Garmin eTrex, or as an app on your smartphone, such as the Ordnance Survey app OS Locate.

183. GPS is one of those items where you get what you pay for, and the credibility of the supplier/manufacturer is paramount. Choose one that you pay for. It makes life easier, and in a safety-critical situation can save a life. There are 'free' apps out there. These are at best useless for giving you a position, and not at all accurate for logging the miles either. A walking party will have at least one of these apps in their midst, generally in the hands of an elderly lady whose grandson downloaded the app from t'internet. It comes with everything you could ever want: distance, height, time, speed, adverts and cut-price funeral plans. It will be the source of all arguments at the end of the day regarding how many miles were actually walked.

184. Switch the device on before you set foot on the route. Let it settle down and get locked on to the satellites. Some devices will be quicker than others at this. Devices that use SD cards for mapping will take longer to get up and running. It is worth leaving the card out until the device has locked on to the GPS system, then inserting the card and waiting for it to load.

185. If you have lots of routes stored in the device, it will load those too, and add time to the start-up. Save your old routes on a computer and then delete them from the device.

186. Once the device is powered up and locked on, save your position as 'Home' or 'Car'. That way you will be able to navigate back to your start point if that is where you need to be at the end of the day, should anything go wrong and you lose your track record.

187. Don't forget to set the device to record your track before you set off on the walk.

188. If you have downloaded a route from a mapping service or content provider, make sure the route has loaded completely before you begin the walk.

189. After 100 metres of walking, stop and check that the device is running correctly, and make any adjustments necessary, like switching it on.

190. Navigate just as you would with a paper map. The only real difference is that you now know exactly where you are without having to think about it. Somehow that just seems wrong. But it is progress, so I am told. You can also key in a grid reference to walk to and the device will guide you to the location.

191. On cold days, wear gloves that can be used with a touchscreen device to save you having to take them off.

192. Set GPS devices to use coordinates that are in the same format as the map you are using, to save having to do complicated transpositions.

193. Don't be obsessed with quantity rather than quality. The number of miles walked and the amount of ascent achieved are insignificant compared to a view of a beautiful stag or a sensitive conversation with someone who has become a new friend.

194. The Ordnance Survey app OS Locate can give you an accurate six-figure grid reference and it is free to download.

NAVIGATION (106-208)

195. If you are out walking using OS Locate, you can send a text message to someone to tell them exactly where you are.

196. If you are using a digital map to navigate with, make sure it does not freeze on you, leaving you in the middle of nowhere with no idea where you are. Keep checking at intervals that it is still logging your position accurately.

197. If you need a fix on your location, let the unit settle down and get a firm lock on the position. This can take a few minutes.

198. Do this experiment. Place the device down with full sight of the sky and set it on 'record track'. Leave it for ten minutes, and do not move it. At the end of the ten minutes, have a look at the log of distance travelled and see if your device has recorded any distance. It will have done. This happens because of the way GPS works using triangulation. If you want to accurately record the distance walked and ascent, place the device in hibernation mode when you stop for any significant amount of time such as lunch. Don't forget to take it out of hibernation mode again afterwards.

199. The more data points you log, the more accurate your recorded track and information will be. But more data means more power consumed, so be careful.

200. If you have a handheld device, rechargeable batteries are best. Carry spares, and always use the type recommended by the manufacturer.

201. If you are using a smartphone to navigate with, make sure you carry a power pack and lead to recharge the battery.

202. Experiment with using your smartphone in low-battery mode to see if it affects the operation of the app. If it doesn't – and it will for some – then make sure the phone is in this mode, to conserve the charge.

203. You can take other measures to conserve battery power on smartphones. Turn off roaming to reduce the phone hunting for a signal and using power. Turn off apps that you don't need to use. Go into airplane mode to reduce battery drain. Keep the phone close to the body to keep it warm and the battery good. Make it secure so if you have an accident the phone is safe on your person.

204. Make sure all electronic devices are fully charged before setting out for a walk.

205. Keep electronic devices dry, even if they are waterproof.

206. Keep compasses away from battery-operated devices in case they affect the magnetic field.

207. Never ever use Google Earth or Google Maps or any such application to navigate in remote places with. It will not end well. Save these apps for going to the shops.

208. Don't become reliant on digital map devices. One of the things digital maps do is remove that immediate connection between you, the map and the wider landscape. This is a real thing, and the outdoor experience can be much reduced because of it. Paper maps give us a wider connection to the landscape – they cover a bigger area in a single view for a start. But laid on top of that is our interpretation of the land and the image on the paper. I believe only paper maps can do this. Digital navigation devices immediately place that connection in the hands of someone else, someone who is not there. We place technology between ourselves and the environment, and then we abandon our own reasoning and hand over the day completely to the little marker on the map.

Navigational tools.

Valleys can be useful for establishing your location when navigating. *© John Coefield*

Be prepared for adverse weather conditions.

STAYING SAFE (209–276)

'Completing a walk is not the goal. Getting home safely is.'

STAYING SAFE (209–276)

BASICS (209–230)

209. To walk safely, human bodies need to be conditioned to the environments they are walking in. The best way to do this is slowly and under controlled conditions. Many walkers come unstuck by tackling a route that is beyond their fitness, experience and knowledge base. It is one of the big issues with how outdoor access is structured, particularly in England and Wales. There are few areas in Britain that we cannot gain reasonable access to by car. Nothing in the journey to the start of the walk prepares us for that first change in environment.

210. Conditioning mind and body to a new environment takes time. People call for Mountain Rescue at night when they are lost on their first trip on Kinder Scout because they have made some basic mistake, usually not taking a torch. But why would you take a torch if you have never walked in the dark? How do you know what it feels like to walk across a field or through a forest in total darkness, with the cold air falling around you and the sounds of the world fading into the background? Walking with a torch at night, somewhere local but away from residential areas, begins to teach you what it feels like, so you start to gain the knowledge of what you need to do to safely walk in the dark. You can condition your body and mind to any circumstances using this technique.

211. Considering the number of people who walk in the outdoors, injuries are not a commonplace event. When they happen, they are generally the result of a chain of small and seemingly unconnected incidents. The accident chain begins away from the hill before a walk has even started. Rushing about trying to find socks, pack sandwiches, fill a flask and remember everything to put in a pack is not a methodical, measured process, and places pressure constraints on people, diverting minds to other things.

212. Pack your rucksack the night before a walk, using a checklist, best written down and left on the rucksack for when you leave. Prepared food for the day can be stored in the fridge. Write DON'T FORGET FOOD AND DRINK on the checklist. Lay out clothing. In the morning, rise early, check the weather forecast and travel news, shower, breakfast and get dressed (changing any item as the weather requires). In winter, check for road closures and transport connections. Leave in plenty of time.

213. Before setting out from home, leave a note, or send a text message to someone, about where you are going, the basics of the route. and when you expect to be back. Put your phone number so that if the unforeseeable happens and someone has to give your details to emergency services they don't end up in a fluster trying to remember your number. Keep it really simple: *Going to Fiddlers Green, Round Hill, Shepherds Meeting Stones, return to Fiddlers Green. Back home by 2 a.m. 07700 900952*

214. Be wary of posting your plans on social media, particularly if you will be away for several days. This can invite unwanted attention to your property.

215. Ensure that all battery-operated devices are fully charged, and you have spare batteries stored safely in a container where they won't discharge.

216. Download the grid reference app OS Locate from Ordnance Survey (***www.shop.ordnancesurvey.co.uk/apps***). This will give you an accurate six-figure grid reference. A word of caution: if you are using the app to call for emergency services, allow the device to settle and use the 'share' button to send your location grid reference. Give as much detail as possible of your surroundings, where you were walking to, where you set off from and how long you have been walking.

Poor visibility on Kinder Scout.

Walking is always popular, especially at weekends.

217. If you do not feel confident in using mapping references, download the location app what3words (***www.what3words.com***). This app divides the world into three-metre squares, naming each individual square with three unconnected words. These words can then be used by anyone with the app to find that specific location. What3words is used by many emergency services now, so call responders are used to getting that information. Again a word of caution: always allow the device to settle first to give an accurate location, use the 'share' button on the app to send the three words to avoid any confusion over the spoken words, and give as much detail as possible about the location, where you began the walk, where you were walking to and how long you have been walking.

218. Carry a spare phone that is switched off. Put it in a safe but accessible place. Store phones so that their screens are not facing out towards the ground, to save them breaking if you have a fall.

219. Have **ICE** (**I**n **C**ase of **E**mergency) as a contact in your main phone. Set the number to someone you would want emergency services to contact.

220. Register for the Emergency SMS Service by texting 'register' to 999, then following the instructions in the reply. Often in areas where there is poor phone reception a text will get through.

221. Always have the essentials: map, compass, food and drink, weatherproofs, emergency shelter, torch, whistle, phone, notebook and pencil.

222. When you get to the start of a walk, take your time to get your kit ready so that you don't have to keep adjusting things as you set out on the route.

223. Paying attention is the best way of avoiding injury. That little stumble, the lack of fluid intake, the wrong direction, the rushing, the leaving the path to take that shortcut to save time – all have the makings of something that could go wrong.

224. Be aware of the signs of someone beginning to struggle: *mumble, grumble, stumble, tumble*. If someone is showing any of these, stop, take a break and get some food and drink into them; if they are diabetic, get them to treat themselves. Rest, then restart the walk, keeping an eye on their progress. If they continue to cause concern, get off the hill and get help.

225. If you take regular medication and need to carry it with you, put it in a container and keep it somewhere safe. In the same place, keep a note of any medication you are taking and at what intervals it is administered. Let someone with you know about this.

226. If you become lost, stop, think, discuss it with a group, or with yourself if on your own. Think it through methodically. If you can't figure out where you are, get back to a known point.

227. Getting separated from a group is common. If it happens to you, stay where you are and wait for the group to come back to you. Listen out for them and use a whistle to attract their attention. If no one shows up, go back to your starting point. If you don't see them before you head home, make sure they know you are safe.

228. If the way ahead seems dangerous – a raging river, a snow cornice, cows in a field – assess the situation, discuss it with any group members and if necessary, look for an alternative route. If there is no alternative, consider turning back.

229. If you feel things are beginning to go wrong, stop and have a brew. Appraise your situation and try to identify the cause of your concern, then decide what you need to do.

230. Completing a walk is not the goal. Getting home safely is.

WALKING WITH A GROUP (231–239)

231. If leading a large group, write down the number of people in the party and the names of any people you don't know. Check that you have the same number in the party at regular intervals. Getting back with fewer people than when you started is a problem you do not want to have.

232. If you are leading a group, tell them how often you plan to stop for comfort breaks and snacks, so they know when a rest stop is approaching.

233. When coming to a crucial turn, wait for everyone to catch up before leaving in another direction, to save people becoming separated and lost.

234. If a group is ascending a rocky gully, stay close together to prevent people below being hit by falling rock.

235. Don't allow the group to stretch out too much, especially in forests. This will prevent you losing the back half of the line and having to go back to find them.

236. Keep the walk within the abilities of all members of the party. Outline the route, giving details of any sections that might cause concern – for instance, an exposed ridge or a steep rocky descent. Let the only surprises be the views. Never force someone to commit to a section unless they are comfortable and have the required skill to do so.

237. Don't leave for home until everyone is off the hill and safely back at the rendezvous point.

238. If you have waited for someone to catch up with the group, don't set off again as soon as they reach you, leaving them behind. Let them have a rest too.

239. If you are leading a group of walkers, you don't always have to be at the front. Move around the group. This way you get different conversations, and you can keep an eye on how everyone is doing.

FIRST AID (240–253)

240. Attend a first aid course with St John's Ambulance, the Red Cross or an independent provider. Book on a course that deals specifically with first aid in sports or outdoor activities.

241. Always have a basic first aid kit. The aim of the kit is to ease the burden on injured people. You aren't going to cure anyone, but you can stop a bleed, support an arm, ease a blister. Bandages, plasters, blister pads, antiseptic cream and over-the-counter painkiller are really all you will need and all that you can use on the hill.

242. Have a stash of safety pins in different sizes, some Velcro, and a length of duct tape rolled around a pencil.

243. If you are waiting for emergency help for an injured person, keep a note of their pulse and breathing rates at regular intervals. Then hand the note to the rescuers. It will give them important information and aid their actions in treating the injured person.

244. Wear a watch where you can see it, so you can easily make a note of timings.

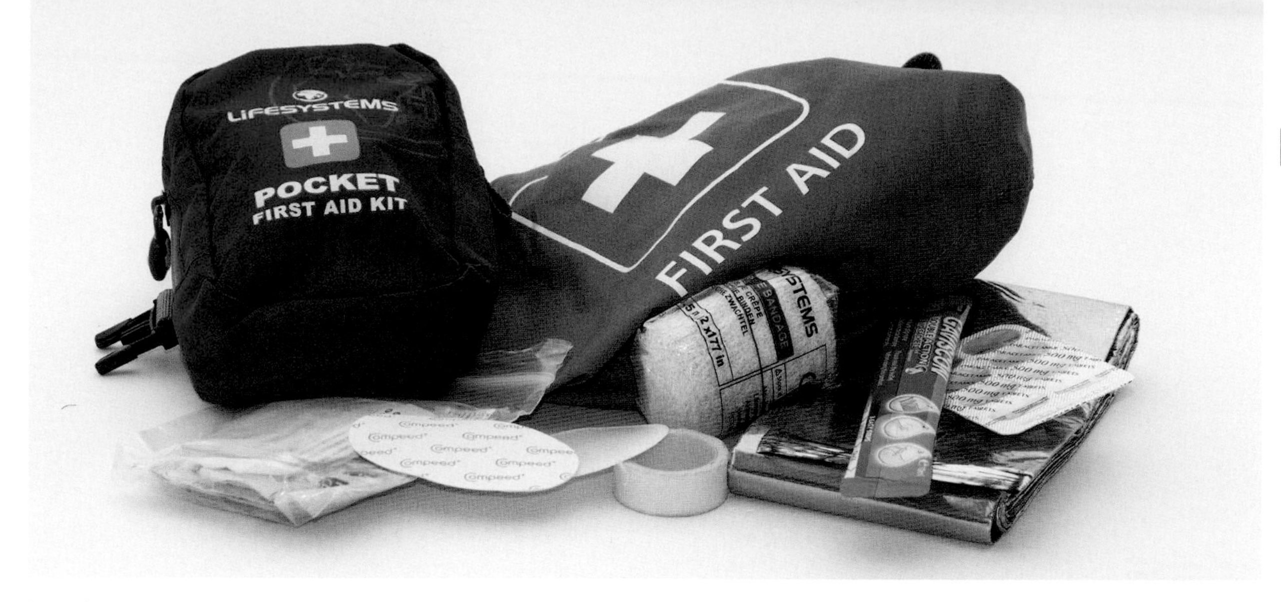

A small first aid kit should suffice.

245. If you have to treat someone for an injury and look after them, talk through what you are doing as you are doing it. It gives them some information and helps you keep a good line on what you need to do next.

246. Knowing what happened is important because it can give you vital information about how to progress with care. For example, if a person has fallen and banged their head, you want to protect their cervical spine as much as possible.

247. If a slip results in a skin puncture that is bleeding, cover it with a bandage and apply pressure to the wound area to stop the bleeding. When the bandage is soaked through, cover it with another bandage but don't remove the first. Do this several times until the bleeding stops. If it has not stopped, remove the dressings and begin again with fresh bandages.

248. Before dressing wounds, rinse them with sterilised water from the first aid kit or bottled mineral water. Dab dry and then cover to provide protection.

249. Catastrophic bleeding can be fatal. It needs immediate evacuation to hospital. Falls often lead to serious internal injuries without any external signs. Check for internal bleeding by testing for hardness in the chest, abdomen, pelvis and thighs, and any blood on the floor (known as 'blood on the floor and four more').

250. A triangular bandage is good for supporting an arm or a sprained wrist. If you don't have a triangular bandage, use a coat with the arm supported by the zip closure and secured with safety pins.

251. If someone has suffered a fall, do not move them unless their life is in imminent danger. Keep their neck and body as still as possible until they can be assessed for injuries. Give them space. Don't let people crowd them.

252. If you have to go for help, try to leave someone with the injured person. If that can't be done, make the person as comfortable as possible, in a safe, warm and dry location, and make a note of the grid reference before you go and get help. Go to the nearest place of habitation or a high point where you can get a phone signal.

253. Keep casualties warm, especially from the ground. If they can be moved safely, place something underneath them that can insulate their body.

STAYING SAFE (209–276)

CPR (254–260)

254. Learn CPR – it could save a life.

255. To do CPR correctly on an adult, the process looks violent, but the aim is to keep the oxygenated blood flowing around the casualty's system. After 30 presses, check the airway and give two rescue breaths into the mouth, watching for the chest to rise and fall. If the casualty is not responding, continue with CPR. After a few minutes of beginning CPR, you will probably be sweating from the extreme exertion. That means you are doing it right.

256. CPR can be a long road, especially in remote places, so you need to be sure you can keep it up until emergency help gets there with the right gear. If you have people around you, they can take turns with CPR.

257. Take note when passing through local communities whether there is a defibrillator, sometimes in a phone box or on the wall of the village hall. If you need one, you can send someone for it if there are people around.

258. Follow the instructions on the defibrillator unit – it will tell you what to do. Get someone else to apply the electrodes as CPR is continued. Do not stop CPR until told to by the machine. Do exactly what the machine says.

259. In cases of hypothermia, you're not dead until you are warm and not breathing. Cold and not breathing means there is a chance.

260. Once the emergency crews get there, let them take over, but wait until they tell you to stop CPR.

GETTING HELP (261–271)

261. If you need help, NEVER phone Mountain Rescue direct, as the bases are invariably unmanned. ALWAYS call 999 and ask for Police/Mountain Rescue. If you can't get a call through, use the Emergency Text service (*tip 220*).

262. Dial 112 to call the emergency services abroad. This number also works in the UK.

263. If you are with a group, divide things to do between the party: someone getting the grid reference, another making notes, a third on the phone.

264. If you need the emergency services, have the following information ready:

- Location: write down the grid reference and/or what3words.
- Nature of the emergency.
- Name and age of the casualty and severity of their injuries.
- When the injury occurred.
- How many people are in the party.
- Anything else you feel might be important: medical history, etc.

265. Keep the phone line you are using to contact the emergency services free. Have other people make calls to family members, etc. on a separate phone.

266. If you don't know your location, think of the last place you are certain you were at, and give this to the emergency contact, telling them which way you were heading or where you were heading to.

267. Always have a torch and a whistle. The signals to attract attention are six short flashes of a torch or blasts of a whistle in succession, followed by a one-minute interval. Light can often be detected much sooner than sound, even in daylight.

268. Keep everyone together while you are waiting. Check that people are warm and protected from the weather. Always carry an emergency shelter to protect people from the elements.

269. Try to station someone in a place where they can guide the emergency services to the location of the casualty.

270. If a hospital visit is required, cars may need to be relocated. Make sure you have any keys for people spending time in hospital.

271. Be prepared to move off when the emergency services have finished their treatment and are ready to transfer to a hospital. Your help may be needed to carry the casualty.

IF THE WORST HAPPENS (272–276)

272. If things don't work out, then you need to think about the living: the people who the casualty was with, particularly loved ones, other members of the party, any bystanders. You have all just witnessed a traumatic event, so it is not the time to go rushing off, carrying on with the day. Gently move people away from the site to allow the crews to do their job. Get people to have a drink, and some food if they can. Allow people to process it in their own way. Begin to think about how to proceed.

273. If a walking partner suffers a fatal incident and you have no phone signal, you will need to leave them to raise the alarm. Cover them as best you can, take a grid reference and time, then work your way off the hill to get help.

274. Be careful when leaving the scene of a fatality. Take your time – there really is no rush, and your own safety is now what is important. Try to attract attention if you see people.

275. Seeing or being part of a traumatic event does strange things to the mind. Some of these happen quickly, while others take hours, days, weeks, months or years to process completely. Talk to someone about how you feel. Don't keep things inside. Most importantly, think about yourself. You might not feel the effects of a trauma immediately, but they will be there. Be gentle with yourself and others. For some, suddenly breaking down in sobs is a natural reaction to trauma and the emotional shock it brings about. Don't fight it. Have a really good cry. If driving, take some time to just settle yourself first. Keep the speed way down. If necessary, get someone to come and pick you up.

276. After an incident, thank people, and later make a donation or send a gift: money to Mountain Rescue, chocolates to hospital, praise to people's bosses.

Pause before you get to the top to stay out of the wind.

Look for the acorn symbol on National Trails like the Cleveland Way. © *Cameron Bonser*

004

WALKING LONG DISTANCES (277–390)

'Walk the seasons. Woodland in autumn, pasture in spring, coast in summer, high mountains in winter. And any other combination.'

WALKING LONG DISTANCES (277–390)

DAY WALKS (277–302)

277. Day walks are the most popular way of getting outdoors for some exercise and refreshing of mind and body. Each of these may be a single walk that starts and finishes at the same point (the most popular), or a linear walk that starts at point A and ends at point B, using public transport or cars to deliver and collect people. Multi-day walks string together several linear walks into one long journey. Day walks can be enjoyed at any time of day, and even at night.

278. You can easily plan your own route, or use a guidebook, or download a route online.

279. Do shorter day walks in winter when the light is limited and weather can be poor.

280. Epics, those '35 miles in a day' walks, are for summer and perhaps the young. Older people tend to suffer, usually not in silence.

281. The easiest day walks follow a known route that is well signposted and has stops for eating and drinking and generally enjoying a slow pace.

282. The hardest day walks are in winter across windswept snow-scoured moors or mountain ranges, where the walker is completely battered by the elements and the mental stress that they place themselves and others under.

283. Both the easiest and hardest walks can be just as enjoyable.

284. Day walks are perfect for that last-minute decision to get out to look at nature. Walk with friends, take a picnic. They make taking advantage of good weather, or making the most of bad weather, an easier choice.

285. A 10-kilometre walk can take all day or a few hours, depending on what the terrain is like – the Cuillins on the Isle of Skye as opposed to the Yorkshire Dales, for instance – and what there is to see.

286. If you can use public transport, then look at this as the primary mode of travel. If you travel by car, then the start of the walk is where you can exert some community spirit. Car-share to save the planet and reduce parking. If there is a car park, use it, even if it means spending a fiver. It helps keep roads clear and hopefully funds local initiatives.

287. If you have to park on the road, park safely and with consideration. Local communities don't want to feel overwhelmed with cars. If a place is crowded, find somewhere else to walk.

288. Never park across access on to fields and tracks. Farmers may need the access, and so might emergency services.

289. Always use a map, paper or electronic, to navigate with. It is rare, but the maps in guidebooks can be wrong, as can directions – telling people to turn left and walking them into a reservoir, for example.

290. A good guidebook will have routes that have been walked by the author, not just drawn from a map. This means that the detail should be accurate and that notes on things to see are worth paying attention to.

291. Squeeze stiles and ladder stiles can be cumbersome to get through for people with limited mobility, so take note of that when planning a walk with a group. A good guidebook will have lots of detail about what to expect. Try, if possible, to avoid such obstacles when you have a large group or members of a walking party with mobility restrictions.

Head out with a walking companion.

WALKING LONG DISTANCES (277–390)

A scenic lunch break on a coastal walk.

292. Always check a stile for stability before using it. Broken stiles can be reported to the local authority. If a public right of way goes over a stile and there is an open gate close by, always use the stile – it saves the exasperated landowner from jumping up and down.

293. If a path crosses lots of boundaries set close together, such as in the White Peak where there are lots of narrow fields, this means there will be lots of stiles to get over, which will add time to a walk. This is particularly useful to know if you have a big group and need to be at a pick-up point for a certain time.

294. As a rule of thumb, close all gates behind you. If you see a farmer working in a field with an open gate, leave the gate as you found it. Many gates have strong springs, so be aware of people following you and hand the gate to them rather than letting it go. If you have to climb over a gate, use the end where the hinges are. It saves the gate from dropping.

295. Early morning walks, before sunrise, to the top of a hill to watch the day breaking are a magical thing to experience. Having breakfast while the land awakens, then setting out on a day walk to be completed by mid-morning with an early lunch in a local cafe, is a fantastic way to see things anew.

296. In summer, try to time a walk so that you are not out in the open with no shade at the hottest part of the day.

297. One of the best things to do in summer is to sit beneath the shade of a tree and just watch the landscape. Oak trees can be found by many walls.

298. The well-known routes will be crowded at the weekend and especially in summer. Try less well-known routes or walk on a weekday.

299. Day walks are good for saunters – from the French *saunterre*, to describe an amble or a leisurely walk. There is no need for an objective. It is sufficient to just enjoy being out and moving through a landscape, perhaps in conversation with friends, or quietly alone.

300. There is sometimes a tendency to carry too much on a day walk – a pack for all seasons and eventualities. Try going out for a walk on a fine day with just what you stand up in. Lowland walks are very good for this because they are generally near to civilisation and therefore amenities. See what it feels like. It might make you feel vulnerable not to have a pack full of gear. It might make you question what you want out of a walk.

301. Check out weather reports the day before and on the morning of the walk. Heavy rain may mean swollen streams and rivers to cross. Hot, dry weather means sun protection and water to carry. Before you leave home, make sure you have everything you need.

302. The most difficult part of any walk is setting out from the start. It is worth checking the map and compass so that you walk off in the right direction and along the right path. It might feel like amateur hour to do this, but it can save an embarrassing walk back into the car park when you realise that the direction of travel is the opposite way.

MORE TO EXPLORE (303–320)

303. Day walks are perfect for exploring the local area around where you live. Have a look at the green spaces that surround you on an OS map and begin to explore.

304. Walk the seasons. Woodland in autumn, pasture in spring, coast in summer, high mountains in winter. And any other combination. Coast-walking in winter can be sublime, in the true sense of the word.

305. It is perfectly acceptable for a walk to follow a route to an objective and return the same way. This is great for summer evening strolls.

306. Circular walks are the most common – after all, don't we need to get back to the car? But we rarely do them in the opposite direction, becoming stuck in the groove of our first outing. Going the other way round opens new vistas and things we missed from the opposite direction.

307. UK national parks have people, businesses, roads and development, which makes them far removed from a wilderness experience. But there are corners where you can get away from it all. With that comes the responsibility to look after these places. People should never be able to tell that you have been there.

308. Work out a local route based on a theme, such as history, geology or natural history. Doing this gives us a greater connection to the landscape and communities.

309. Find out about local festivals and customs, such as Well Dressing in Derbyshire, and choose day walks that take you through the villages on these days to experience the heritage.

310. Studying the geology is a great way to engage with the landscape. Buy a geological map to show you what ground you are covering. Harvey and British Mountaineering Council maps have this information included.

Plan things for children to see, like the Wizard of Whirlow in Todmorden.

311. Look out for old stone bridges and clapper bridges across rivers and streams. These are often indicative of old packhorse routes and can lead to some wonderful vistas.

312. You can gauge the age of a place by the pattern of walls that are around the houses. Close to the dwellings, if there are long thin fields stretching all around, this indicates a medieval community. As the fields get bigger and squarer, this indicates enclosures from the 16th century onwards. At the top, the long walls and massive fields show enclosure from the 19th century.

313. Learn about Sites of Special Scientific Interest (SSSIs). These areas of land are of special conservation significance for wildlife, flowers, mammals, etc. Try to avoid encroaching on these areas as much as possible. If unavoidable, move carefully across the land and don't leave a trace of where you have been. Some areas are fenced off to help restoration or protect a fragile ecology. Don't venture into these areas unless authorised to do so.

314. Download apps to help identify trees, wild flowers, butterflies and anything that takes your interest.

315. Foraging should always place wildlife first, so don't pick clean, leaving nothing for the birds and mammals. When foraging from nature's larder, always leave plenty for others and for wildlife.

316. Never pick wild flowers; leave these for other people to enjoy.

317. For family walks, let the children plan some of the route. Call it their route and let them lead it on the day. There is no better feeling than guiding someone to a location. That is a real achievement for a child.

318. Download the coordinates of local geocaches for children of all ages to find. Learn about the letterboxes that are out in the mountains. Leave a letter for someone else.

319. Occasionally have a day walk with the purpose of clearing away litter. Take a bag and a litter picker and walk down a path where you have seen too much rubbish. Clear it up and either take the litter home or leave it by a bin and tell the council you have left it there for pick-up.

320. If you come across fly-tipping, lots of litter, old camps, etc., take a photo and a grid reference, then send these to the authority responsible for the land.

TRAIL WALKING (321–341)

321. Trail walking, long-distance walking, multi-day walking, backpacking – a long walk is just a series of day walks, one after the other.

322. Self-supported trail walking is one of the better ways to experience the more remote areas of Britain.

323. There are 16 National Trails in England and Wales. The 15 existing trails range from 79 miles long (Yorkshire Wolds Way) to 630 miles long (the South West Coast Path). The 16th trail will be the England Coast Path, as yet incomplete.

324. The oldest National Trail is the Pennine Way, starting at Edale in Derbyshire, and finishing in Kirk Yetholm in the Scottish Borders. It is 268 miles long and can be a test of endurance, stamina and skill. A winter route along this trail is not for the faint-hearted.

WALKING LONG DISTANCES (277–390)

325. Scotland has 29 Great Trails, ranging in length from 24 miles (Dava Way), to 214 miles (Southern Upland Way). In addition to these, the 537-mile Scottish National Trail begins in Kirk Yetholm and ends at Cape Wrath, so you could walk from Edale in England to the tip of Scotland.

326. The National Trails website (***www.nationaltrail.co.uk***) and Great Trails website (***www.scotlandsgreat trails.com***) are full of information about all these trails and other local trails that are nearby.

327. The National Trails in England and Wales have an acorn sign at points along the way to ensure that you are on the right path. The Scottish Great Trails use a thistle logo.

328. Each National Trail has a certificate of completion that can be obtained from the National Trails website.

329. The National Trails and Great Trails are an excellent way of exploring new parts of the country. If you normally walk on the moors or in the mountains, walking along a coastal path can be an exhilarating experience.

330. Most National Trails and Great Trails are walked in summer when local facilities are open. Spending money in local shops is a good way of helping independent retailers and local communities.

331. Sherpa services exists on some trails. These companies will transfer much of your baggage between stops, leaving you free to enjoy the trail with a lighter pack.

332. Maintenance of the National Trails is carried out by volunteers; this is a good way of giving something back.

333. The country is criss-crossed with thousands more trails. OS maps show the more popular trails, such as St Cuthbert's Way to Lindisfarne along the border country that straddles England and Scotland.

334. Many local trails can be joined up to make a multi-day walk, using local B&Bs, campsites or hostels as stops.

335. One of England's most popular trails is not even a National Trail. The Coast to Coast route – from the Irish Sea at St Bees in Cumbria on the west coast to the North Sea at Robin Hood's Bay in North Yorkshire on the east coast – follows the route outlined by Alfred Wainwright. The 182-mile route is largely free of signposts, relying almost entirely on OS maps and good navigation skills.

336. Trails are often linked to a theme – for example, the Gritstone Trail follows the geological journey and landscape of the Pennines. Many trails are linked to history, like Hadrian's Wall Path or Offa's Dyke Path. Some are pilgrimages, such as the North Wales Pilgrim's Way.

337. Trail walking is great for family days out, especially with young children.

338. You can string a series of day walks together to complete a long-distance path. This is useful if you need to save holiday days for family gatherings.

339. Splitting long-distance trails into manageable stages means that you can have a full-on series of adventures with the whole family.

340. Make a list of trails you would like to do and tick off at least one per year.

341. Some great trails are:

- Pennine Way (England) – 268 miles
- Offa's Dyke Path (Wales) – 177 miles
- West Highland Way (Scotland) – 96 miles
- Tour du Mont Blanc (France, Italy and Switzerland) – 105 miles
- GR11 (Spain) – 510 miles
- GR20 (Corsica) – 118 miles
- Kungsleden (Sweden) – 270 miles
- John Muir Trail (USA) – 211 miles
- Milford Track (New Zealand) – 33 miles
- Everest Base Camp (Nepal) – 80 miles

TRAIL-WALKING LOGISTICS [342–390]

342. A trail can often be shared with other users, such as bikers and horse riders. Always pay attention when walking along a trail for people coming up from behind. Keep to the left and say hello as you pass people to make the walk more pleasant and less stressful for all.

343. Trail walking can be combined with overnight stays in hostels, B&Bs or hotels. This might mean walking off the trail at the end of the day to your accommodation, and back again the next morning. Make allowances for this in your schedule.

344. Trail guides such as the Big Trails series from Vertebrate Publishing (***www.v-publishing.co.uk***) are a great way to get inspiration and an overview with information on the route, accommodation and points of interest.

345. Completing a long route requires a level of fitness that is above what you would need for a day walk. Build up slowly over several weeks and months for a big walk. Do not succumb to the fallacy that you will acquire the fitness on the trail.

346. Begin trail walking on shorter walks. Start with a two-day walk, including an overnight stay, and walk back to the beginning. Then a trail of moderate length, say a three- or four-day walk, then a week or more.

347. Begin a trail walk with low mileage, building the daily distance covered over the days until your body is used to it.

348. Don't force the walk. This is the easiest way to pick up an injury. Let the walk unfold and allow your legs to find their own way.

349. Long-distance walks require both stamina and resilience. Develop these before you begin that journey along the 268-mile Pennine Way, or the 2,653-mile Pacific Crest Trail in the US.

350. Walking long distances means you will almost certainly have a mixture of weather – be prepared for this. Not taking waterproofs on the West Highland Way because it was sunny back home in Hounslow is not a good decision.

351. The more remote the trail, the harder it will be. The terrain will be less accessible and will have fewer defined routes. This can sap the energy of any walker, so make sure you prepare well beforehand. Plan in days of rest on multi-week walks.

352. Remote walks like the Cape Wrath Trail can have significant challenges, particularly in bad weather. Make sure you have conditioned yourself before attempting these.

353. Have a plan for if it all goes wrong. How will you get yourself and your stuff home?

WALKING LONG DISTANCES (277–390)

354. If you are walking a trail with a friend or a group, be prepared for relations to become a little strained. When the tension rises, be gentle with each other and yourself. Keep conversations light and help each other.

355. A walk has many stages for the mind to contend with. It starts with hope and maybe a little trepidation, then progresses to a well-worn comfortable groove, before reaching the end with a little impatience and perhaps some sadness that it is finishing. Learn to anticipate these emotional swings and adapt your mindset.

356. Weight is crucial on long-distance walks. Too heavy a pack can ruin a walk before it has even started. Too light a pack can restrict the walk due to lack of food, weather gear or shelter.

357. Weight is a major factor in whether a walk is something to be enjoyed or endured. Try to keep weight down by using low-weight but high-calorie food.

358. On long trails, mail home the stuff you don't need.

359. Try to not carry water for any significant distance. Collect water for a brew or cooking half an hour at most before you stop. This saves you weight.

360. Either boil all the water or use a filter to take out any nasties before consuming it.

361. Take water from a fast-flowing source and check upstream for any animals that are lying dead in the water.

362. Walking in wet weather for several days can play havoc with your feet. The skin can swell and begin to break down. This is a time to pay particular attention to them to prevent injury.

363. Wet socks can be dried by wringing them out and placing them over your sleeping bag.

364. Carry a small absorbent towel to dry you at the end of a day's walking.

365. Camping is a good way of walking trails, although it does mean carrying more kit. Try it on a two-day walk and see what you need to make the walk comfortable.

366. In England and Wales, it is illegal to wild camp in most parts. Dartmoor permits wild camping in certain areas. In Scotland, you can camp almost anywhere, but some places do have restrictions.

367. If you are walking a trail and using a tent, then the logistics become more important. Working out where and when you can replenish your supplies to reduce the amount of food you need to carry is one of the most important aspects of a long-distance walk.

368. If you see a cafe or a pub, try to get to it to have a hot meal and some food that doesn't taste as though it came straight out of a packet. A burger, chips and salad (for health), followed by apple pie and ice cream, washed down by a pint of ice-cold pop, is sublime after a week of eating noodles and nut bars.

369. If you are camping, try to get to your spot in plenty of time so you don't have to set up in the dark.

370. Always choose a flat spot that is not in a dip where water can collect. This way the tent or bivvy will not get waterlogged.

Camp on Bleaklow in the Dark Peak, Derbyshire. Always aim to set up the tent before nightfall.

371. Develop a system of habits at the end of a day. Setting up a tent, putting a brew on, taking off your boots, resting with a cuppa, sorting the dog food, sorting your own food, changing into night gear. Whatever it is, work on it until it becomes second nature.

372. If you are using a tent, place wet gear in the vestibule to keep the living area dry and clean.

373. Keep a set of clothes dry for putting on at night. A cheap pair of plimsolls are good for wearing around camp. A big pair of baggy woolly socks are amazing on the feet after a day of walking.

374. Always change out of your dry night clothes at the start of a new day and put on your walking gear.

375. Put on a different pair of pants every day. Take two pairs and wash a pair out each evening. If it isn't raining the next day, dry them on the back of your pack.

376. Toilet facilities need to be well away from the campsite and watercourses. Practise packing out, by bagging up human waste and tissue into a sealed container for disposal once you get to civilisation. If packing out is not feasible, make sure solid waste is buried away from sources of water, and paper is burnt if safe to do so. Do not set fire to vegetation.

WALKING LONG DISTANCES (277–390)

377. Sphagnum moss is a great toilet product and the best way of dealing with that dab or smear technique. It also leaves the personal bits feeling great. Don't forget to remove any thorns or twigs, before and after use.

378. Have a clear bottle in the tent with you at night, so you don't have to get up and out of the tent to have a pee. Use a wide-mouth bottle and wrap some coloured grip tape around it to stop it slipping out of your hands. Close the lid tight after use. Easier for men than for women, true, but on a stormy wet night anything is possible.

379. If you are cold, a water bottle with fresh pee tightly closed and held between the knees is a good way to warm you up.

380. In the morning, dispose of the contents well away from the camp.

381. Never drink from the pee bottle. Unless you are a TV personality. Or wannabee.

382. If you have a dog with you and the weather is bad, settle the dog down in the tent after it has been dried and has eaten in the vestibule. Always take a dog toy, but not a squeaky one.

383. Take a notebook and pencil to record your experience. Set time aside for jotting down things you see, making sketches and noting details of people you have met along the way.

384. Set your camera to number photos from zero – that way you will have an accurate photographic record in order when you upload the images.

385. Make the first photo your ID card, giving your name and contact number, so that if you lose your camera and someone finds it, they can contact you to return it. Offer a reward.

386. Always make sure you turn your camera off after taking a photo.

387. Take enough image storage and battery power to last the journey.

388. Plan where you can recharge items, staying in accommodation for the odd night if you are mainly planning on camping, to enable you to access power.

389. Always ask a cafe if you can charge items, don't just assume. Be responsible walkers.

390. Leave the laptop/iPad, worries, career, football results and unfinished DIY project at home.

Take the opportunity to learn about local history.

An autumnal forest walk at sunrise.

Enjoy the 'purge' as you ease into a walk.

005

WALKING ENVIRONMENTS (391–619)

'If you are new to walking, get your body used to moving across uneven terrain, and up and down hillsides. Walking on different surfaces, like grass, rock and soil, trains the feet and ankles to become more flexible.'

Walk from the city into the countryside.

WALKING ENVIRONMENTS (391–619)

URBAN WALKS (391–414)

391. We don't think of walking around an urban environment as an activity, probably because it is something we do almost daily, without any preparation or thinking. But it is something we should do with a purpose occasionally. I think walking in our own locale or visiting another urban setting engages different areas of our brains from the ones that get engaged on a hill or mountain. And that's a good thing.

392. The urban landscape hides the sense of a space. Buildings sit on contours hiding their shape and form. Hard boundaries, those roads and pavements, rail lines and car parks, force us along a certain path. This is deliberate in many cases, the planners wanting to separate human from machine. But the planners also want to guide us towards or away from spaces. Think of the central shopping areas in cities, how easy it is to find yourself in the large wide spaces that can accommodate the maximum number of people – or shall we call them customers, as that is what city centres were designed for in the latter part of the 20th century.

393. Look at a map of your own urban area and see what shape it is. Look at it on a street map, then a topographic map, then a satellite map image.

394. Urban walking is about a landscape of human interaction and direction. There will be parks and woodland, and those strange edgelands that sit between town and country, which we used to play in as children but forget about when we become adults.

395. What we forgo in big skies and wide-open spaces with no one other than ourselves there, we replace with history, culture, architecture and anthropology. Urban is the human landscape and there is a reason for everything. We just have to take the time to look.

396. Urban adventure is a great way of getting children involved in walking. Add in a park or a museum, or a walk by a river or canal, to bring new experiences to their life.

397. Choose a day that will be easy weather-wise. This is not the time to be out in a great rainstorm. If that happens, you will probably seek refuge in a cafe or pub, which on reflection is not such a bad idea!

398. Wear comfortable shoes or trainers and easy loose clothing.

399. A jacket is good. I mean an ordinary jacket. The thing about urban walking is not to look like you are on the way to Everest Base Camp. This is carefree walking, the arms unencumbered by straps and plastic, the feet held in loosely fitting shoes – shoes, mind you, not great clumping boots. Jeans are good (fancy advising going out in jeans, in a walking book!). Or these lightweight trekking trousers that look like ordinary daywear. The thing is to blend in, but perhaps be original.

400. Blending in helps you to observe – that is the point of an urban walk. Dressing for show is for parties or picnics in the park. What we need is to pass through the urban landscape unnoticed.

401. Don't be loaded down with kit. A small pack or shoulder bag to hold a drink, some food, a notebook, camera, phone. Or just walk out in what you stand in, with perhaps some change in your pocket or everything on your smartphone.

402. Try some psychogeography, allowing the geography of place to guide you on the walk. This means casting aside any personal wants and focusing instead on what the geography of a place is saying and how that is influencing you.

WALKING ENVIRONMENTS (391–619)

403. Step out of the house and begin to walk and keep walking. Carry some money for coffee, food or transport back home. Carry a notebook and pencil to make notes and drawings of your experience. Use your phone camera to take photos and videos of things that interest you. Look for connections such as street names, street ephemera (*tip 408*) or ghost signs (*tip 409*).

404. Walk during the week and you get the bustle of business: the deli, the sandwich shop, the cafe. This isn't a time for shopping, so don't head into the nearest department store. Use only the shops that can sustain your expedition, like the food dumps that Shackleton laid across the ice on his way to the pole. The shops we want are fuel dumps: food, information, culture, people.

405. If you have the facility, use an app such as OS to track your route without having to keep looking at a map. Urban walking, ironically, is about being free of directional control, so allow yourself to observe what is happening around you and consider how that influences you.

406. It is the play that is enacted in front of you that is important in urban walking. And it has acts: early morning is when the landscape is waking, with the street cleaners, the delivery drivers, the people on their way to or from work. Come 9 a.m., the centre is bustling on the fringes, cafes come to life, independent shops begin to open, pocket parks start to be colonised by people, old and young: mothers with babies meeting for their daily escape from home, elderly people taking their constitutional. At lunchtime, it is all bustle: sit outside a cafe or in the window and watch the world go by as people rush to eat and meet and then get back to the essentials of doing nothing of great importance. As evening falls, the centres empty their teeming activists who have hidden behind curtain walls and chain store aisles. The glow comes when the lights are switched on, the yellow spreading beyond the windows, pulling people in to meet and eat and share their lives, for a moment at least. Then night-time and the shadows lengthen the buildings, cloaking them in darkness, as though they too were temporary. Sit quietly and watch, for the fox and her cubs doing the rounds of the bins down the alleys that thread, unseen by humans, behind the facades. Take in the silence, broken by the odd drunken shout from a too-late drinking session.

407. Old maps can give clues about what the urban environment was used for before it was built over. It is interesting to visit sites today to see how the past resonates with the present. Search the National Library of Scotland digital archive (***https://maps.nls.uk***) for maps of local areas.

408. Street ephemera is all around us, even some that you will find out on the hill. The Ordnance Survey benchmarks that surveyors use to measure the land can be found in abundance. Look around the old churches and bank buildings, or bridges or posts – they were placed in positions that were thought to be permanent, at least for a lifetime. There are over half a million benchmarks, taking the form of a chiselled arrow below a horizontal line set about one metre above ground level.

409. Shadow buildings and advertising signs abound. The imprint of long-gone and forgotten buildings and advertisements can be found on gable ends all over a city, giving tantalising clues of how we used to live.

410. Walk from urban areas right out into the countryside. It might be a long way or take just a few minutes, but do it. Notice how the environment changes and what effect that has on you. In the urban space, we are closed in, measured, placed. In the countryside, we often have the illusion of space, when in fact we are corralled and guided this way and that.

Urban design: Arts Tower, Sheffield.

Visitor centres have a wealth of useful resources.

WALKING ENVIRONMENTS (391–619)

411. Walk back into an urban environment after spending time in secluded countryside. Take note of any effects it has on you: what you see and hear, and how that affects your personal sense of well-being.

412. Take a bus journey to the end of the line. No one ever does that unless they live there. Be an explorer.

413. Develop a day walk that is close to home, so that you don't have to use a car. It should be a walk that will take you an hour or so, that you can get out to at least once a week. Do it each week, at the same time. Make notes on what you see, who you see, what people talk about. Note how the landscape changes week by week. Take photos of the same spot, view or tree, to see how the year works out in nature. Use this period to immerse yourself in an environment that is far removed from your everyday. Many urban areas have woodlands that are full of birdlife, so take some binoculars.

414. Be careful of traffic. Lost in your own reverie, it is easy to step out at a junction into the path of a vehicle. Humans are least visible in an urban environment.

LOWLANDS (415–457)

415. The fields and valleys are a good place to begin country walking, learning what works and even finding out if walking is something that you enjoy. Country parks with large open spaces are ideal for beginning the process of hillwalking. Walking locally means you don't have to get specialist equipment or clothing. Your normal daywear will be sufficient.

416. Lowland walking includes a much more human landscape of fields, boundaries, rivers, farm pasture, communities, roads and easier access.

417. If you are new to walking, get your body used to moving across uneven terrain, and up and down hillsides. Walking on different surfaces, like grass, rock and soil, trains the feet and ankles to become more flexible.

418. Tourist information and national park visitor centres are to be found in the larger communities. Here you can find lots of information about local walks, along with transport, accommodation and general points of interest. Visit your local library to get information about your area. Look at history, wildlife and any events that are taking place.

419. In national parks, ranger offices will have a wealth of information on what is happening locally, including information on footpaths, wildlife and events. Rangers can advise about any walks you want to do in the area.

420. Guidebooks are a good way to explore an area. Many books will have a series of walks ranging from a few miles up to a full day's walking distance, and offer a variety of walking experiences.

421. This landscape can be a great way to discover the history of an area. You will also encounter more wildlife and flora and learn about natural history. Study how villages were built with local stone, and factor in time to visit landscaped estates, great country houses and famous parklands. Look at local history sites for information about the area. Search the local library and archives for material. Check websites for local Wildlife Trusts, RSPB nature reserves and wetland reserves so you can go on nature and wildlife walks.

WALKING ENVIRONMENTS (391–619)

422. Plan things for children to see: a cave, stepping stones, newborn lambs. Engage children's minds in what is happening around them as you walk along. Take reference books to identify flowers, wildlife and history. Local visitor centres often have free leaflets on what you can see in the area.

423. Lowland areas are often a repository for geocaches. These make superb navigation exercises, with the added thrill of a find at the end of the rainbow. They are a great way to get young people involved in walking outdoors in any weather. Search ***www.geocaching.com/play*** for locations.

424. The lowlands are often where you will find camping sites, barns, hostels and a whole range of accommodation that you can access to make a weekend of walking in a new area or support a longer-distance trail walk. Be aware that camps will be busy on bank holiday weekends.

425. Fields and valleys are a good place to learn how to use a map and a compass. There will be easily identifiable features that you can match map and terrain to. Stand in one place and hold the map so that it corresponds with the terrain around you and is pointing in the direction in which you intend to travel. Practise identifying features – for instance, a stream junction, a wide track, a road and buildings.

426. Take a map and find a place to sit so that you can study what all those lines and symbols mean. Identify features on the map, then go and see what they look like on the ground.

427. Develop your skill level with techniques such as 'handrailing': using a boundary – which could be a fence, a hedge or a stone wall – to get to another location.

428. Practise 'pacing': knowing how many double steps you take to cover a known distance. Lowland trail walks often have distance markers every mile or kilometre. This is a good way to establish how many paces you take to walk 100 metres and a kilometre.

429. Before setting off from your starting point, make a note of its location so that you can easily return to it when you need to.

430. Using a mapping app can give you an accurate record of the distance you walked, how much ascent and descent was gained, and how long the walk took. It can also give you information about your walking speed at any part of the route and how long you stopped for. This information can be invaluable when looking at new walks or ways of improving your walking.

431. Walking is popular, so you will come across a lot of people. Choosing less busy times, such as during the working week, can give you more space to explore and practise. Try out new things such as gear or experiencing what it is like to walk in bad weather, with a group or on your own.

432. Lowland walking is a good place to begin if you have restricted mobility. Lowlands often have excellent trails and access points for a variety of users. It is worth contacting the landowners, council, National Trust, etc. to see what facilities are available, and where to find easy-access routes.

433. Forest walking is a superb way of experiencing a different environment. The wider trails provide easy walking and allow you to observe the trees and wildlife.

434. Forest trails can be used by walkers, runners, horse riders and bike riders. Share the trail, giving each other room.

435. If you are walking with a dog and see a horse rider ahead, bring the dog to heel or put them on a lead so the horse does not feel threatened.

436. Spend time sitting in trees, either at ground level or in the tree branches. It is one of the best ways of connecting with nature.

437. Forests often have information boards that will tell you what birds, wildlife and plant life can be seen.

438. It is easy to become disorientated in a forest, so always make sure you know how to exit the forest at the end of your trip.

439. Mapping apps won't always work in forests due to tree cover. If you need to get a location, move to open ground.

440. Check national forestry websites for details of trails and events.

441. Walk the coast. You can get lower than the shoreline in parts of Eastern England, and you can walk below sea level. Some of the best walks in Britain take in sections of coastline. If you are near the coast, walk along the beach and dip your toes into the water.

442. Never ever attempt to walk across quicksand, even if it means a huge detour. Morecambe Bay, for instance, is well known for its casualties.

443. If you are walking in Cornwall, visit the Tidal Observatory at Newlyn. This is where the datum line for every height measurement in the country comes from. The numbers on the OS map contour lines and spot heights come from here. This is ground level.

444. Be low impact. Lowland walks can often be started straight from home. Walking from the front door into the countryside opens a whole new way of experiencing what is on your doorstep.

445. Travel out by bus or rail to a stop, then walk back home. This gives a new perspective on a landscape – the anticipation in the journey out, the relaxed walk back, not having to be at a station or bus stop for a certain time to get home.

446. Go to the end of the line, where few people venture, and explore what is there.

447. Plan a walk to a local event, making it the halfway point of a circular walk. This means you will arrive on foot, giving a different feel to the day from driving in a car. Save the environment, save money, exercise and relax.

448. Local walking groups are a good way to begin walking or exploring areas you have just moved to. Pick a walking group that focuses on something you are interested in or perhaps has members of a similar age to you.

449. Join the Ramblers (***www.ramblers.org.uk***) and support their work. They also run weekly walk programmes with walks of differing lengths for people with a range of abilities.

450. Join the British Mountaineering Council (***www.thebmc.co.uk***) and get involved with hillwalking groups in your local area.

451. If walking in a group, wait until everyone has gone over a stile or through a gate before walking through with a dog. This way, no one can trip on the dog lead, and you don't have to rush.

452. Be careful near farmyards if you have a dog. Farm dogs are very protective of their home and the livestock and can become aggressive when they see another dog. If necessary, when a public footpath passes through a farm, stop and see if all is clear, call out to see if anyone is around and tell them you are passing through with a dog and ask them to keep theirs away. If you see a farm dog being aggressive and there is no response, find another way around the farmyard. At all times, protect all animals and humans.

453. Always dispose of dog poo responsibly. Never ever leave a bag of poo hanging from a tree or thrown at the side of the path.

454. Cows can be very inquisitive when they see a dog and begin to run towards you. If you feel threatened, let the dog off the lead – the cows will follow it and the dog will outrun them. But be wary if you are near a road – don't risk the dog running out into oncoming traffic.

455. If you come to a field of cows and don't feel safe, find another route around them, particularly if they are in a field with a public right of way. You have a right to be able to walk safely.

456. When walking along roads in lowland areas, always choose the side of the road that gives you and the driver the longest view, even if that means crossing the road a few times. Better to be seen than to end up in a ditch.

457. Winter walking in lowland terrain can be wet and muddy, and that means more slips and trips. Take more notice of the ground in front of you and where your feet are going.

UPLANDS (458–512)

458. Many upland areas have open access and comply with the requirements of the CRoW (Countryside and Rights of Way Act) 2000. This gives the public unfettered access on any part of the landscape, meaning that the walker is no longer constrained by a public rights of way network but can, if they so desire, walk anywhere. There are restrictions, with camping generally not allowed without permission of the landowner, as well as days when the moors are closed to public access. But these areas offer some of the finest walking in Britain.

459. Open access means you don't have to keep to the public right of way but can walk anywhere within the access area. These are shown on OS maps as a shaded line enclosing the limits of the land. Always use access points wherever possible and try not to climb over stone walls and fences. On fenced access land there should be a stile every 100 to 200 metres along the fence line.

460. Grouse moors often have restrictions on use, particularly dogs. Dogs and walkers can legally cross a moor if it is on a public right of way. Landowners can legally refuse access to dogs other than assistance dogs anywhere else on the moor. Landowners can also close a moor to public access other than public rights of way several days per year. To find out about moorland closures in England, visit ***www.openaccess.naturalengland.org.uk***

461. The uplands of Britain are characterised by a wildness and remoteness that creates a feeling of isolation and solitude. As such, the landscape requires a sustained and proficient engagement to allow a walker to appreciate the special qualities of this environment.

Watch out for over-inquisitive cows.

462. Upland landscapes begin above the treeline. The area between the last trees and the skyline is often covered in large patches of bracken, beyond which runs a line of crag or steep hillside leading up to an unseen moorland plateau or hilltop.

463. The space between upland and lowland terrain is often filled with ancient woodlands, streams and crags. This is where you may well find the most diverse wildlife, particularly birds and mammals.

464. Because of the remote environment, upland walking requires good planning, ensuring that you have the skills and equipment required to stay safe and gain a fulfilling experience.

465. Upland walking requires a reset of our mind. Think about what most of us do when we go for a walk. We leave our comfortable, familiar cocoon of a home, travel in another comfortable and familiar cocoon of a car, then get out and rush into the hills, dragging along behind us everything from our daily lives. Like warming up our muscles, we need to reset our minds so that we can become attuned to our new and not-so-familiar environment.

466. Take notice of the 'purge'. It is probably one of the most important aspects of your walk. The purge is where we let go of our daily life – whether it is town or country doesn't matter. A good way of doing this is during the slow approach into a route; it is especially effective on upland walks and multi-day hikes.

467. Prepare the night before for a day or several in a remote area. Leave a plan of the route and important items such as keys, money, map and phone somewhere that you will have to pass in the morning, so you don't forget them.

468. Always have a map and compass, first aid kit, survival gear and appropriate clothing.

469. Pack food for the walk the night before, even if it then has to be kept in a fridge, so you don't have to do this in the morning and can concentrate on getting ready – unless making the food in the morning is part of your methodology for a day out on the hill. Make sure you carry sufficient food and liquid to sustain you, and always have a little more for that emergency stop. Chocolate, sweets and jelly babies can help in all situations.

470. Methodology. Ritual. Habit. Methodology is the system we develop to ensure we have a good day. Ritual is the individual part of the system of methodology. Habit is the ritual being part of us in each environment. Develop this process for your walking so that you are efficient and perform at the peak of your ability. Doing this removes the things you have to think about when you could be studying that interesting rock formation up ahead. For example, to get across a featureless moor to a certain point, you might use pacing, counting each double step (Methodology). After each 100 metres travelled you might call out '100 metres', '200', and so on, and perhaps move a bead up a piece of string so you don't lose count – and keep doing that until you reach your location (Ritual). You might do this as a matter of course because that is the easiest and simplest way of reaching your destination (Habit).

471. In an emergency, rescue teams can take a long time to get to a casualty in an isolated environment. Being self-sufficient, by being prepared, is the best way to cope with any adversity that may be encountered. Upland walking can be isolating, and the mind needs to be prepared for this.

472. A combination of tough, relentless terrain and significant isolation can have a serious detrimental effect on days out in upland areas. Condition your mind and body by building up the time spent on the high moors until you become attuned to the landscape and the weather.

473. Distances on moors can be deceptive. Experiment with how long it takes to walk a kilometre over different terrain. Use a normal pace; don't try to beat a clock. Try both a direct route and a route covering a longer distance but over easier ground.

474. Quite often the quickest and most efficient route is 'the Old Man's Route': a circuitous route between two points that uses the contours of the land and easier ground. Old men, such as me, use this to conserve our energy and prevent any injuries. And it is usually quicker.

475. Often you will encounter lost holloways – tracks worn deep into the land by the passage of feet over centuries – and sled ways – sloping ways descending a hillside made by sledges being brought off the moor during peat and stone extraction. These ancient ways are a good way of getting up on to the moortops. They are easily identified in winter snow as a depression in the snow cover.

476. Where the terrain sweeps up to the moor plateau, take your time and zigzag your way up the hillside to conserve energy.

477. Navigation skills need to be much more acute in upland walking. There are fewer man-made objects to navigate by.

478. Learn to distinguish between tracks, footpaths and sheep trods. Following a narrow black path, neatly cut through the heather, for a long way often results in you being miles away from the path when it turns out to be a sheep trod.

Holloways are ancient tracks that may be found through woodland.

Distances on moors can be deceptive.

479. Having said that, a sheep trod can be a good way of getting across upland terrain. Sheep will generally take the easiest route to conserve energy.

480. Thighs, knees, ankles, calves and, most importantly, lower back all take a hammering when walking across a moor without paths. Condition your body beforehand for the abuse you will be putting it through.

481. A moor has short grass or long grass, heather or bracken, rocks or peat, dry ground or boggy ground, visible streams or hidden gullies. You must be able to cope with and know how to deal with each of them.

482. Moving in and out of peat bogs is an art that can only be practised in situ. The skill lies in being able to identify the small clumps of grass that form solid ground. Aim for these. They might even hold your weight.

483. Walking poles help hugely in upland walking. They aid in ascent and descent, help to keep you upright across boggy terrain, and test the depth of that innocuous-looking patch of peat.

484. Is it bivi or bivvi or bivvy? Sleeping outdoors is what I mean. If you intend to camp away from a designated camping area, always ask permission of the landowner. For a camp on the moors, set up camp above the last wall line, away from civilisation, arriving late and leaving early.

485. It is impossible to leave no trace of our presence. Even walking will leave footprints. We can minimise the impact we have on a landscape by leaving a site as we found it except for the trace of our tent or bivvy. Do not move stones, cut down trees or start a fire. This all disturbs the ecology and wildlife of the area. Pack out all waste: human, dog and food.

486. Choose a site near water so that you don't have to carry it in over a long distance.

487. Never have an open fire on a moor, at any time. The moors can easily catch fire, even after a period of wet weather, and the higher location means that winds can drive fire across moors at an alarming rate.

488. Shooting butts are great for getting out of the wind for a brew. But be wary on entering that someone hasn't 'used' them.

489. Take binoculars to spend time watching wildlife on the moors. The curlew, snipe, buzzard, kestrel, sparrowhawk and merlin are all there to be seen. On the crags and swooping down into the valley you may find the peregrine falcon.

490. The mountain hare is a special joy to see during winter, its white coat shooting across the moorland. These elusive creatures can suddenly spring up out of a deep grough, stare at you, then shoot off. Keep a keen eye out and report any sightings to local nature conservation bodies.

491. Groughs (Peak District), haggs (everywhere else) and gullies (the unsuspecting) are slices into moorland. Some can be as deep as thirty feet or more; others are less than head high. The deeper ones generally have a stone floor with a small stream running down the centre. The water has worn away the peat down to bedrock. These can be a corridor for crossing a moor, although navigation will become challenging.

492. Learning how to walk up and down a steep-sided slope in a grough made of what appears to be chocolate fondant is a skill once mastered never forgotten. The best way is like walking down a slope loaded with snow, digging the heel in to form a platform to support the (hopefully) upright human body. Confidence is everything.

493. Some of the best entertainment is watching a friend trying to extricate themselves from a peat bog or grough. They may well ask for help. Don't rush in. Desperation levels need to reach panic point. There is still enough time to sit down and take out a flask of hot coffee and perhaps some chocolate – a Tunnock's wafer is my favourite. Then relax and enjoy the show. Offer words of advice based on your own experience, and others can also join in. The more differing advice the now trapped and expletive person gets, the more annoyed they will become. Wait until they begin flailing their arms around wildly, their red face smeared with the deep dark-chocolate coating of wet rancid peat, small sprigs of heather plastered to their skin and eyes, the hat long gone and now soaking up water far below them, steam beginning to seep out of their expensive and now ruined Gore-Tex waterproof jacket, as the heat they have built up begins to overflow along with their patience and sense of composure. When all these have been achieved by the hapless group member, move forward carefully – you don't want your shiny new gaiters and boots to get dirty – and with a reassuring air of calm, ask if they need assistance.

494. Coming upon an area of lovely short vivid-green grass after yomping across a moor trying to avoid grass tussocks and leg-breaking hidden gullies is a thing of pure joy. Firm ground to walk on, perhaps a rock nearby to rest and have a brew, take in the scenery and check the map. These small islands of rest can be used as transit points when crossing a moor. Keep your eyes open for them.

495. Not all vivid green bits of moorland are islands of safety. Some are bogs of sphagnum moss, which at first glance look like solid ground, but will not bear the weight of a single boot. Beneath that glistening bright green is a void filled with water and dead animals, liquified peat. Its depth is bottomless, one foot thrusting down with the forward momentum of your body while the other foot remains on dry ground several feet above. This is groin-stretching and hamstring-straining at its absolute best. It ruddy well hurts. Avoid at all costs.

496. Long grass that spreads out like waves and looks like a reed bed with defined edges signifies water. A trickle of water will be heard from somewhere hidden in the grass. These are the braided water routes that fan out across a moor until the water rejoins and finds a course as one to the river below. Be wary: this is leg-trapping, leg-breaking territory. Your foot suddenly plummeting down a void, the boot filling with water, a sharp stone gouging out a furrow in your shin. Onward movement risks snapping the shin like a dried chicken bone. The use of walking poles and eyes is of great help here.

497. Long grass also means tussocks: the tall, fan-shaped clumps of grass that seemingly sit on a small mound. The unwary will try to walk across the top of these, as what lies between them is dark and sometimes invisible and may just hold a braided stream. This is an enormous error, as trying to balance on a precarious clump of grass is a recipe for a broken ankle. The best way to walk across such ground is to slow down and place the feet between the clumps of grass, always testing that the ground is firm and accepting the fact that this will add minutes if not hours to the journey.

498. Heather moorlands are highly managed environments structured to cater for the breeding and growing of grouse and livestock. But they are also home to cotton-grass, sphagnum moss, bilberry and cloudberry. Keep an eye out for these jewels in the landscape.

Take care with foot placement on heather moorland.

Restrictions on grouse moors.

499. Heather is burnt to promote the growth of young shoots, and this creates the patchwork look of grouse moors. The burning produces a thick acrid smoke that chokes the lungs and can travel long distances. If you encounter this on high ground, consider altering your route to avoid the direction the smoke is travelling in.

500. Heather is grown in stages, each of a different height. Understanding this allows a walker to move across a moor using the shorter heather. Where heather has been burnt, the terrain is bare. Navigate across a moor using these areas of naked land. Choosing shorter heather to walk through goes some way to protecting the nests of ground-nesting birds from disturbance. Try to avoid walking across moors at nesting time.

501. Bracken hides the hidden threats of holes and rocks. In summer, when the bracken is high, it is impossible to see down to the ground and the risk of injury is significantly increased. Tall bracken is difficult to get through. A route around the area may be further but will take less time and be less tiring in the long run.

502. Bracken is home to the tick, which can attach itself to human flesh and cause Lyme disease, a serious affliction that can last for years and be very debilitating. Whenever walking through bracken or heather, always check for ticks on exiting. If you find any, use a tick-removal tool immediately and treat the area with antiseptic.

503. Wearing gaiters for walking across heather and bracken will stop material getting inside footwear and save shins from being scratched. After walking through heather or bracken, check that laces have not come undone.

504. If you end up in a peat bog, your boots and lower legs coated with thick slimy peat, walk through mid-height heather afterwards to clean all the peat off.

505. Stay clear of boulder fields that are covered in high bracken. They require balance and a slow pace to make sure you don't slip and break a leg or become trapped between boulders.

506. On grouse moors, watch out for wire snares placed in the long grass along animal trods to capture predators. Be wary around stink pits (pits filled with dead animal carcasses that you can often smell from far away) for snares and keep dogs well away from the area. A foot or a paw can easily be caught in the loop. It is illegal to interfere with legally placed snares and devices used to control predators.

507. If you are challenged on a moor and you have a legal right to be there, no one can make you leave.

508. Never venture on to a shooting moor when it is closed and there are shooting notices up, unless you are on a public right of way, in which case you have a right of legal access. Make your presence known before crossing and wait to be told that all is safe.

509. Prior to visiting an area you are unfamiliar with, check access websites and Ministry of Defence (MOD) restrictions.

510. An area surrounded by red arrows on the map signifies MOD land and can be subject to closure. Never ignore warning notices. Artillery shells really hurt. When walking across MOD land or land formerly used by the military, never pick up anything that might look like an explosive device. And watch where you put your feet.

511. If you are wild camping in former military areas, do not pick up something metal to knock tent pegs in with. I once went up to check on an apprentice who had been sent out to reset a fence post only to find him knocking it in with a small mortar shell. I shouted to him – from a good distance – to gently put it on the ground and walk away.

512. Be very wary of entering a secure area on MOD land. Places like Fylingdales on the North York Moors are heavily guarded with cameras and patrols. Never stray from the legal footpath.

MOUNTAINS (513–559)

513. Mountain walking requires extra skills, strength and stamina. These are best built up slowly over time. You can only get mountain legs by putting them on the mountaintops.

514. It is rare that a walk starts at the top of a mountain. Time will be spent walking in, sometimes over rough terrain, before the ascent begins, with a long slog to the top. Allow for longer days or plan shorter walks.

515. If you are planning on doing a lot of mountain walking, improve your stamina by running when not in the mountains. This helps improve cardio performance and strengthens leg muscles. Strengthen your core, lower body and legs to help you move easily through mountain terrain.

516. Use Naismith's Rule to assess how long you will need to be out on the hill. Allow one hour for every five kilometres walked, plus one hour for every 600 metres of ascent.

517. Adjust Naismith's Rule to your own circumstances. If you walk an average pace of four kilometres per hour and take ten minutes longer to ascend 600 metres, alter your timings. Make it personal to you.

518. Write out the route and put down the times when you should be at certain points.

519. Always have escape routes planned into your day in case you need to quickly get down into the valley.

520. Choose routes that fit with the ability of the least experienced member of a walking party. There is no sense in frightening someone for the sake of a little excitement.

521. Choose footwear wisely. Wear what works for you and ensure that it is appropriate for the terrain and the wear and tear that mountain walking can cause to equipment. This is not a place for flip-flops.

522. When loading a pack for a mountain walk, make sure that it is in balance and fits well. Keep the pack close to your body, with heavier items stored in the middle and back of the pack to distribute the weight more evenly.

523. Leave the alcohol at home. Water, tea, coffee and hot chocolate are all good in the mountains.

524. In Scotland, never ever forget your midge net. You will only do this once.

525. Particularly in cooler months, carry more clothing in your rucksack than you will necessarily need. Walk in cold. Wearing fewer layers at the beginning of a walk helps you find the right temperature balance for your body, the terrain and the weather. When walking uphill, think about removing layers to prevent overheating. You can add extra layers if necessary once the exertion has ended to maintain a comfortable environment next to your skin. If you use a layering system, vent the inside regularly to prevent the build-up of moisture.

Snowdonia slate. Studying the geology of an area can be fascinating.

526. Weather can change quickly in mountain environments. Use the Mountain Weather Information Service (***www.mwis.org***) and the Met Office website (***www.metoffice.gov.uk***) to gain a broad view of the weather in the coming period.

527. Being aware of the weather is an important mountain skill. Get used to looking at the clouds to see the weather coming towards you. A basic way of doing this is to use the crosswinds rule. Stand with your back against the wind at ground level. Look up at the clouds directly above your head. If they are moving left to right, the weather will deteriorate. If right to left, it will improve. If straight ahead or behind or staying still, the weather will stay the same. This is good for the time period immediately in front of you.

528. You don't want to be in the mountains in a lightning storm. Try to get out of the mountains – or avoid going into them – if you are aware of possible storms. If you are caught out in a lightning storm, do not shelter under a rock or inside a cave, where the space between rock and ground acts like a spark gap with you as the conductor. If there is no alternative, get into open ground and sit on your pack to insulate you from the ground.

529. In hot weather, try to time walks so that you are walking in the cool part of the day or in shade.

530. Use high-factor (50+) sun protection. Pay particular attention to the backs of the knees and the neck.

531. Always make sure you have clothing that can cover exposed skin. Wear full-length lightweight shirts that also give sun protection.

532. A floppy hat with a wide brim gives better protection than a baseball-type cap.

533. The higher you go, the colder it will become. Carry extra layers of clothing and extra food. On Ben Nevis you can expect freezing temperatures at any time of year.

534. Ridge walking needs experience. Try using a guide for your first walk or two. Crib Goch in Snowdonia, Striding Edge in the Lake District, and the CMD arete and Aonach Eagach in the Grampians are all serious knife-edge walks.

535. Never walk across a ridge in high winds – it is far too easy to get blown off.

536. If you are trapped by high winds, try to get below the ridge line to a place of safety.

537. Always know where the crags are. Identifying these on the map and being able to navigate around, through, up and down them is an important mountain skill.

538. Learn the difference between a sheep/goat trod and a human route. It saves getting cragfast (stuck so that you can neither ascend nor descend safely).

539. Always ensure that the way forward can be reversed to prevent yourself from becoming stuck.

540. Learn how to balance your body when moving through rock.

541. Be careful when walking down a steep mountain path. Keep weight above your centre of gravity and feet firmly placed to stop them from sliding away from under you.

542. Become a hill bagger. Bag the Munros (in Scotland) and Furths (in England, Wales and Ireland), which are the mountains over 3,000 feet.

543. Become a trig bagger. Ordnance Survey triangulation pillars stand on many mountaintops. The highest is Ben Nevis.

544. Walk the Three Peaks: Snowdon, Scafell Pike and Ben Nevis. The total ascent is over 3,000 metres, with a distance from the summit of Snowdon to Ben Nevis via Scafell Pike of around 450 miles. Leave the car behind.

545. Being in remote areas means you are much more susceptible to bad consequences if things go wrong. Always have backups for things: spare laces, phone, batteries, food, maps, etc.

546. Always have an emergency shelter to cater for everyone in the group and any dogs.

547. Mobile phone signals are hard to get in the valley, but you often get 4G on the summit. Save the social media posts for the summit and that all-important mountaintop selfie.

548. I find that I burn at least triple the number of calories on a mountain walk as I do in the valleys. For a day of walking, I need to be looking at replacing around 300 to 400 calories per hour, depending on the total height gained, speed of walking and steepness of the terrain. I need to carry at least 2,500 to 3,500 calories of food.

549. High-density, high-calorie foods give the best calorie-per-gram weight ratio for mountain walking. Nuts, dates, pork pies and chocolate all have high calories per grams. Fruit will be low in calories and weigh much more.

550. Small amounts of high-calorie food eaten at regular intervals throughout the day are much better than one meal.

551. High-energy foods like jelly babies can give a short-term boost for that steep ascent.

552. Hydration is critical in a mountain environment. It helps keep the thought processes working. Make sure you drink regularly and have enough for you and any dogs.

553. Take a filter to use in mountain streams so that you can drink on the go without having to carry excessive amounts of water.

554. On hot days, a little salt added to a bottle of water and fruit juice can replace some of the salt lost through sweating.

555. Consider adding a sports additive powder with electrolytes to your water to replace lost salts and minerals in your body.

556. If you are heading out into the mountains and know the day will be hot, freeze two 500-millilitre bottles of non-carbonated drink the night before and carry these in the centre of your pack. That way they will stay cold for much longer and give you a much-needed boost on a hot day.

557. Mountains seem to compress time. Keep an eye on your watch.

558. Make sure you take a torch and extra batteries in case you become benighted (as in overtaken by darkness, not in a state of moral ignorance!).

559. If you're planning an overnight camp, walk in late and walk out early. Bivvy near the top – that way, you get the sunset and sunrise.

SCRAMBLING (560–574)

560. Scrambling is the bit between walking and climbing. It is great fun. Take it easy, using low-grade gullies to learn the skills needed.

561. Scrambles are graded for difficulty. Grade 1 is the use of feet and just hands for balance. Grade 2 is the use of hands for purchase and movement. Grade 3 calls for rope techniques on some sections.

562. Go on a scrambling course to learn how to use your body, hands, feet and the techniques that are used in this sport.

563. Incorporate scrambling as a section of a walk to give more variety and add some spice to the day.

564. Help protect nature. If birds are nesting on the scramble route, abandon the scramble for another day. Leave the birds in peace. Don't pick wild flowers from a ledge for your loved one. Many rock plants are protected.

565. The golden rule of scrambling is never go forward if you can't retreat. Always have the ability to down-climb a route.

566. Break complicated pitches down into small sections and practise the moves.

567. A firm sole is very useful for getting those edges on the rock face.

568. If wearing a helmet gives you confidence, wear one. Don't be influenced by what others may think.

569. Check each handhold and foothold before you commit to a move when scrambling up a rocky section. What you want are solid holds that will take your weight.

570. Always try to keep three points of contact as you move.

571. Be very wary of rock flakes suddenly snapping as you place your whole life on them. Never grab vegetation for a handhold.

572. If someone is struggling on a section, take a break, climb down to a safe spot, have some food and drink. Then calmly talk through the moves before helping the person to overcome the obstacle. Always have an escape route on any section of a scramble.

573. It is OK to go around.

574. Never take a dog on anything other than the simplest of scrambles. Watch out for dogs cutting paws when scrambling or ripping out a claw.

WALKING ABROAD (575–619)

575. Make sure you have any necessary permits for where you are going. Walking in many countries requires permissions. Places such as Yellowstone and Yosemite in the USA have limits on when and how long you can stay.

576. Don't let your visa run out.

577. Make sure you have had all necessary vaccinations well ahead of the date of departure.

578. Buy insurance that is specific to what you are doing. The British Mountaineering Council have specialist insurance for hillwalking, trekking and backpacking (*www.thebmc.co.uk/modules/insurance*). Make sure you have insurance cover for rescue.

Grade 1 scrambles use hands for balance.

The Tour du Mont Blanc. © *Stephen Ross*

579. Read the Foreign Office travel updates for the region (***www.gov.uk/foreign-travel-advice***). It saves flying into a war zone or falling foul of any travel restrictions, particularly when travelling to parts of the world that are susceptible to some of the more exotic diseases. Record the contact details of British consulates in the country you are going to.

580. Store important contact details online, such as travel companies, travel insurance and local consulate information.

581. Take photos of all your documents and store them online so that you can access the details if you need to, wherever you are.

582. Have the details of your bank with international dialling and account security information somewhere safe and secure, like a password-protected file on your phone, with a cloud backup.

583. Notify your card issuer of where you are going so that they don't block your card.

584. Back up financial stuff. So have two credit cards, not debit: one Visa, one Mastercard.

585. Don't carry all your important documents and money in one place. Spread stuff around so that you always have a backup if something gets lost or stolen.

586. Take a satellite messenger/locator device, like the SPOT Messenger or Garmin inReach, and make sure your subscription is up to date and extends beyond the period of your trip. Make sure you are aware of the costs involved in deploying the device. You don't want to come home to an unexpected bill of thousands of pounds.

587. Long trails can extend across different seasons, so you will need to establish what gear you need. Summer gear is not much use in winter on a high-altitude section. This means you might have to use resupply stations, such as post offices in local towns, for pick-up and return of gear.

588. Speak to the travel company to get all the advice you need to ensure your gear can be transported and will arrive safely.

589. If you can, send items that are not essential and not of significant value by courier to a pick-up point. Many post offices and hotels will accept items if they know you are coming. This saves you weight on the flight and gives you less to worry about during transit. Send stuff a week or so in advance so you can check it has arrived safely. If it does not arrive, you have time to do something about it.

590. Research trails online. Find out if the routes have any diversions in place.

591. If you are using a guidebook, copy the pages you need and take only those with you, or get the book on an electronic reader.

592. When travelling, expect some delays. Take some good reading and be wary of electronic devices that can't be taken on board a plane. Go with the flow. You do not want to kick off in an airport, because that is a guaranteed way to get a quick flight back home.

593. Wear your boots on the flight out. That way, if your gear gets lost, you still have boots that fit well. You can buy more gear, but boots will need breaking in for a long walk.

594. Buy maps locally, so long as you know you can. This saves weight on a flight.

595. Airport information points have lots of good advice. Before you head off where you think you need to be, check with them.

596. On arrival, hit the local supermarket for things such as hygiene supplies and food. Try to get things that have more than one use in order to reduce weight for both walking and travel. Basically, don't buy soap and shampoo – soap will suffice and will lessen the weight.

597. After a long flight, don't jump straight on to the trail. Take a day or two to get used to your set-off point.

598. If your flight arrives late in the day, book into a nearby hotel to rest for the night, then in the morning you will be fresh, things will be a lot more visible and there will be more help around.

599. Comedy does not travel well. Keep the jokes to yourself in official and public places.

600. Pay particular attention to local laws and customs. You can be stopped from leaving a country if there is a criminal investigation.

601. Read bulletin boards for any places you are going and understand the etiquette for a region. For instance, in some countries touching, such as placing a hand on a shoulder as a gesture of kindness, is frowned upon.

602. At religious sites, be careful of how you dress and check whether photographs can be taken.

603. That native piece of artwork will have to be carried home, all the way. Don't bother.

604. At the trail head, talk to the locals to get any advice. Many have ranger stations.

605. Altitude can bring you down low. And can be serious. If you are walking at altitude, make sure you have a slow acclimatisation.

606. If you are trekking with a company, make sure they include time to acclimatise to the altitude and environment.

607. Hygiene is essential when walking in remote areas. Have a fixed cleaning routine to remove the day's walking from your body.

608. Filter, boil and/or treat all water if in remote places.

609. Take a small bottle of antibacterial cleanser and keep those hands as clean as possible.

610. Keep your fingers away from your eyes and nose to prevent infection from something you have picked up.

611. When using huts and hostels, keep your gear safe and in sight as much as possible. Never leave valuables where they can be taken.

612. Hostels, huts and shelters all tend to be very basic, so your mind needs a reset. This is not home.

613. If you are camping, make sure this is allowed in the place where you want to stop. Many trails have designated places.

The GR221 in Mallorca. © *Stephen Ross*

614. In bear country, have a proper food canister and store it well away from the campsite. If bears are in the territory, never eat in the area where you will be sleeping. Learn from the locals.

615. Follow the local protocols for human waste. Some require you to pack all human waste out of an area. Others allow you to dig human waste into the ground.

616. Don't forage abroad. Being dependent on correctly distinguishing what is safe from what isn't doesn't bode well. Watch the film *Into the Wild* (spoiler: it does not end well).

617. Never pick plants or harm wildlife. Many countries have signed up to CITES (the Convention on International Trade in Endangered Species of Wild Fauna and Flora) to ensure the conservation of wild plants and animals.

618. Some people like to walk with others they meet on the trek. It is your walk, and it is OK to say you want to walk alone during the day and perhaps just meet up in the evening.

619. Check in regularly to notify people where you are and how you are doing.

Some walks are more challenging than others. Always choose routes that everyone in a group can do.

Stay clear of crags and snow cornices.

006

WINTER WALKING (620–700)

'Wear appropriate footwear for the terrain and conditions. Generally, winter mountains mean four-season or winter boots with a firm, hard edge around the sole. This is not the terrain for that old pair of trainers and some waterproof socks.'

WINTER WALKING (620–700)

BASICS (620–629)

620. Walking in winter is not the same as walking in summer. It requires an additional set of skills and equipment. The end of many a day has been hastened by ignoring this simple fact. Attend a winter-walking course to learn what you need to do.

621. Some of the best days' walking can be had in winter, with blue skies and the sun beating down, and a feeling of adventure in the bones.

622. On your first few winter walks, take someone with you who has experience. Use a familiar route that you have walked in summer. Keep it short so that you can pay attention to the environment and how you are dealing with it.

623. The daylight is shorter, beginning later, with darkness falling earlier. It is better to walk into the light, setting out in darkness, than to walk into the dark, returning after sunset.

624. In winter, keep walking sections short to ensure you maintain the correct course.

625. Walking in snow can be tiring and consume much more energy. A 16-kilometre walk in winter conditions can take much longer and consume significantly more energy than the same route in summer. Be aware of this and its effect on you and your group. Having a good breakfast and food throughout the walk helps keep the body warm and alert.

626. Beware of wind chill. A wind of around 10 to 12 miles per hour at an air temperature of 0 degrees will produce a wind chill of -10 degrees. Although a wind up to 20 miles per hour won't really affect your progress when walking, it will have a significant wind-chill effect.

627. Learn how to assess windspeed. At 10 miles per hour, the wind will have little effect on you. Up to about 20 miles per hour, you will feel the wind ruffling your hair. At 25 miles per hour, walking will start to become something to take care over. You can get knocked about by the time it has reached 30 miles per hour, so stay away from ridges and exposed lines. At 40 miles per hour, you will be leaning into the wind, so it's time to start getting lower down. Above 50 miles per hour, you need to get off the hill as the wind will start to take your legs from under you.

628. Don't use a hydration bladder in winter conditions. The cold, combined with wind chill, will freeze bladder tubes and mouthpieces, depriving you of fluid. Carry water bottles inside your pack and stop regularly to rehydrate.

629. Take an old technology phone, fully charged but switched off, as a backup. Old phones are easier to use in rough weather, with their push buttons rather than techie touchscreens. Keep your main phone close to your body to maintain a degree of warmth and stop the cold draining the battery.

WINTER GEAR (630–652)

630. If you haven't had your winter boots on in the past year, then it's either been too mild or you need to reappraise your priorities.

631. A good B2 boot, with a stiffer sole, makes it easier to move across snow than footwear that has a more flexible sole, like summer boots or trainers (*tips 898–900*). A stiff base makes it easier to use the edge of your sole to traverse across a slope, giving you security as you move.

632. Stiff-soled boots can play havoc with tendons when spending long days out in winter conditions. Be aware of this and build up the mileage carefully to condition your body.

Spikes can be useful on B1 boots for short sections of ice when lowland walking.

633. For lowland walking and the lower upland areas, spikes are often sufficient to give a good grip when walking along foot-paths and trails that are covered in a mixture of ice and snow.

634. At the start of the winter season, make sure your spikes are sharp. Sharpen them with a file if they are blunt.

635. Practise putting your crampons on at home before you set out for the hill – but not on the wooden flooring in your front room. Learn to put them on in the dark, so your hands get accustomed to the movements needed to ensure that they fit correctly.

636. When on the hill, always put crampons on where there is a level area with something firm to support you. A rock is what you are looking for. Failing that, make a flat platform by stamping down an area of snow.

637. Walk with your feet slightly further apart than usual, especially if it is the first day of winter walking, to prevent crampon spikes catching legwear or boots.

638. Try to avoid walking over large sections of bare rock with your crampons, as this will blunt the spikes and may damage them beyond repair.

639. If you come across a small section of ice on a slope, put the crampons on. A slip can waste significantly more time than the time it takes to fit crampons.

640. If you use over-trousers, wear ones with full-length zips on the leg and always fit crampons after putting these on.

641. If you are wearing gaiters, make sure the buckle is on the outside of the boot to prevent the crampon spike catching it and becoming a trip hazard.

642. Keep crampons in a crampon bag when storing them in your rucksack, to stop the spikes from puncturing clothing, the pack or other items.

643. Always dry crampons after use and store them in a dry place.

644. Before winter begins, clean and waterproof your clothing as directed. Dirty clothing will absorb water. Clean clothing with a refreshed DWR (durable water repellent) coating will repel water and keep you dry for longer.

WINTER WALKING (620–700)

Hoods add warmth but affect hearing.

645. Keep an eye out for bargains in outdoor shops during summer. Don't just look in the walking section – check the snow sport departments. The best over-trousers I have were designed for snowboarding but are great for walking.

646. A hood in winter can make a massive difference to body warmth. But it can reduce hearing, so keep alert for people talking to you.

647. In winter, mittens are a lot warmer than gloves with fingers. Dachstein woollen gloves, an old favourite of alpinists, are amazing, warm and cheap.

648. Waterproof over-mittens add warmth to any type of glove.

649. Fit gloves with tethers that keep them attached to the wrist. That way, you won't drop them or leave them behind when you take them off. If gloves have drawcord closures, make sure these can be operated with one hand.

650. Fingerless gloves or mittens are useful if you need to use a compass or phone.

651. Wear layers. Powerstretch trousers or Ron Hill Tracksters with waterproof over-trousers will keep you warm and dry and give freedom of movement. On your body, wear a base layer and mid-layer, supplemented with a waterproof windproof top as required. Have a selection of gloves and hats and a balaclava in the pack so that you can be ready for any conditions.

652. Always have some eye protection. Sunglasses are a must in winter conditions, as they stop the bright light from damaging the eyes. Goggles are excellent at protecting the eyes from the wind and the cold. They stop the eyes streaming, which can obscure vision.

WINTER SAFETY (653–700)

653. Winter walking in the mountains means ice axe, crampons, helmet, snow shovels, probes and PLB satellite messenger/locator device – as well as all your other kit. Learn how to use all of these before going out in the winter mountain landscape.

654. If setting out for a winter walk in a mountainous area of Scotland, look at the avalanche report before you set out. Information can be obtained from ***www.sais.gov.uk***

655. Learn about the risk of avalanche and how to stay safe. Slopes loaded with snow can be dangerous. Find out more on the Mountaineering Scotland website (***www.mountaineering.scot/safety-and-skills/essential-skills/weather-conditions/avalanches***).

656. Wear appropriate footwear for the terrain and conditions. Generally, winter mountains mean four-season or winter boots with a firm, hard edge around the sole. This is not the terrain for that old pair of trainers and some waterproof socks.

657. A pair of spikes in the pack is always a good idea where crampons are not required. Placed on footwear when necessary, spikes can help with mobility over slippery terrain.

658. Always carry a bivvy tent in winter. Even if the weather is benign when you set out, the conditions on the hill can change quickly.

659. Refrain from walking along crag edges in winter snow. Snow cornices can extend far out from the actual land and offer a significant fall risk.

660. Snow will cover holes and gullies, so take care when walking across open land. This is where good walking poles come in useful.

661. A white-out in a mountain environment can be a scary thing. Definition is lost between the land and the sky, the scene just appearing as a white space. This makes orientation difficult and there is a complete lack of vertical axis. To see whether you are moving up a hill or down, throw a snowball ahead of you. If it disappears out of sight, then the land is falling away from you. If it lands in front of you, you are on a flat area. If it suspends in mid-air, there is rising ground in front of you.

662. In a white-out, the compass is still correct, as it always has been. No matter what your brain is telling you, trust the compass.

663. In a white-out, keep dogs on a short lead so that they don't get lost or go over an edge. Switch on the red light on their collar (*tip 958*). It's also good to have a falconry bell to listen to.

664. Take special care of children when winter walking. Keep checking they are warm and dry.

665. There is nothing wrong with a snowball fight or building a snowman. Make winter walking fun.

666. Watch the weather. The walk may finish well but getting home could prove problematic if the roads have been closed due to snow.

667. Keep stops short and to a minimum. A steady pace with regular stops for refuelling helps maintain a constant body temperature and good progress.

668. Always keep your pack closed to stop snow getting inside and wetting everything. When you stop, take out what you need and then close the pack.

669. If you stop on a snowy slope to eat or drink, place your rucksack loop around the shaft of your ice axe and then fix that into the snow. This stops the rucksack from accidentally cartwheeling away from you down the slope.

670. When descending a snow-covered slope, keep the toe of your boot higher than the heel, so that the heel digs into the snow and forms a small platform to walk on.

671. Try to keep to the path where possible. In winter, paths can become very wide as people try and stay clear of the muddy bog in front of them.

672. Don't walk out on to ice-covered ponds, and keep animals away from the ice too.

673. Watch out for ice on stiles.

674. Always carry an ice axe when walking in the winter mountains. Choose a walking axe with a straight shaft of a length that suits your height. Don't choose one that is too long, as this could hinder you when trying to stop your slide as you plummet down a snow slope towards a precipice.

675. Choose an ice axe with a leash to attach it to your wrist or body. This way it won't disappear after you have dropped it. You will just have a bruised shin.

676. Always walk with the axe pick forward, in the uphill hand, swapping from hand to hand as you zigzag up or down the hill.

677. When not in use, store the ice axe in the bindings on your pack or slide it down the gap between the pack and your back.

678. Learn how to self-arrest (stop yourself from sliding). This is the most important technical skill you can have as a winter walker in the mountains.

679. Use the first day in the winter mountains to revisit training. Practise self-arrest, walking with crampons and ice axe, and moving up and down slopes.

680. Make a small platform at each turn when zigzagging up or down a hill. Stop and take a moment to rebalance and reorientate yourself with the landscape.

681. Conditions can often change quickly in winter mountains. A helmet, while it may seem overkill for the ground in summer conditions, is often the one piece of kit that can give you confidence to get down that long slope.

682. Buy a helmet that you can fit a woolly hat under, and a balaclava. Store it on the lid of your pack. Store your goggles inside your helmet so you always know where the two items are. Make sure the helmet will take a head torch.

683. You don't have to be in the Himalaya or even Scotland for an avalanche to happen. There are several in the Peak District each year. Stay away from steep slopes and overhangs loaded with snow.

684. The best way of locating someone caught in an avalanche is with an avalanche transceiver. The next best way is with a probe pushed down into the snowpack. Practise with this equipment before setting out into a snow-loaded environment. Places such as Aviemore have special parks where you can practise avalanche techniques.

Keep everyone warm, and always keep an eye on the weather.

685. Speed is crucial if trying to locate someone caught in an avalanche. It will take time for rescue services to get there. Do not delay in starting a methodical search of the area.

686. Buy a metal snow shovel; the plastic ones are useless.

687. Learn how to dig a snow hole. Spend a day in the winter mountains just digging out a snow hole to see how long it takes and how much energy you expend. It gets hot digging out a useful snow hole. Pick a decent day to do it in, but imagine what it would be like in a winter storm. Practise using different methods of building. The method I like best is the burial grave. Others prefer caves. Some want to build a shelter.

688. Always mark a snow hole, for people to find you. A walking pole with a bit of tat fluttering from the handle is all it needs.

689. Make the snow hole larger than you think you need. Give yourself room to move around. Take a candle or two and a lighter.

690. When digging, remove as much clothing as is safe, to stop sweat soaking the material and cooling you down once you stop.

691. If you have a dog with you, make sure they are away from the wind and kept warm while you dig the hole. Keep checking on them.

692. Always make sure you have an air hole to allow fresh air into a snow hole so that you don't greet the morning with a groggy head.

693. Make a small shelf to put items on, so that you can find things like the torch quickly.

694. Camping at night out in the snow is a special event for children of all ages. It enhances the senses, the feeling of the raw coldness on skin, the dark sky, the uncountable stars. Make it a goal to do it at least once every winter.

695. Whether in a snow hole, tent or bivvy bag, at high altitude or low, sleeping out in winter is a great way to extend days out. At night, the aim is to preserve as much heat as possible and maintain a good level of comfort.

696. Clothing and sleeping bags don't add heat to your body. They can only keep it in. Therefore, always get into your sleeping bag warm and zip up the collar to trap the heat in.

697. Take a good winter sleeping bag, and an air mattress with a mat for added insulation. Put on hat and gloves, extra pairs of socks, an insulated jacket, thermal bootees. Make a hot drink before you go to sleep. Fill a bottle with hot water and put it in your sleeping bag.

698. If you have a clear night with no expected rain or snowfall, sleep outside on the hill using a good bivvy bag. Choose a spot that is sheltered from the wind and away from dips that will collect cold air. That way, you get to see the winter night sky.

699. Take a hot drink, or better still the means to make a hot drink. Chilli flakes, black pepper and Henderson's relish added to hot Bovril or miso is just an amazing drink. It warms through the body in seconds and leaves a feeling of contentment.

700. Snow is full of air and will take longer to boil than water from a stream because you have to melt it first. Get the brew on in plenty of time before you intend to turn in.

Enjoy a wintry sunset.

Winter walking on Blea Rigg in the Lake District. © *Stephen Ross*

Cooking with a Jetboil Minimo and Flash … and a keen observer.

007

GEAR (701–808)

'Develop a packing system for the rucksack so that you know where every item is and can find it easily in a storm or in the dark.'

GEAR (701–808)

BASICS (701–716)

701. Basic gear: map, compass, appropriate footwear, waterproofs, hat, gloves, rucksack, whistle, torch, small first aid kit, comms device, emergency shelter, sun cream, drink, food. That is all you need.

702. Always take a phone. Put it in low-battery mode and airplane mode to conserve the battery.

703. Smartphones can support mapping apps, can download walks, and more importantly can be interrogated by rescue services to establish location if a connection is available.

704. Have a backup phone. One that uses buttons for the numbers, isn't connected to the internet, has a really long battery life and is waterproof. Switch it off and put it with your first aid kit. Use it only for emergencies.

705. Head torches are a must. But also carry a hand torch and a spare head torch or batteries.

706. Carry a small power pack with lead for your phone.

707. Make sure you have the correct leads to connect a power pack to your electrical gear. Store the leads with the pack. Charge everything before you leave home.

708. Keep electronic gear away from the compass or it might affect the magnetic field.

709. Sunglasses are useful in bright conditions. Not only do they protect the eyes, but they allow detail in the land to come through. Goggles are great for stopping your eyes running in windy conditions.

710. A floppy hat can stop you getting sunburnt and keep the rain away from your face.

711. Head nets are a must in Scotland. You don't want to be without one when the mozzies strike.

712. Don't think walking poles are for the inexperienced. They are excellent at keeping people safely on their feet over rough terrain, and aid ascent and descent. They take pressure off the joints, saving knees and ankles and extending a walking life by many years.

713. Carry some paracord and a few electrical tie wraps to hold stuff together.

714. Carry a small multi-purpose tool, such as the Leatherman, for running repairs.

715. A small roll of duct tape can be used to repair damaged items. A spare pair of laces can be used for so many things.

716. Don't carry an axe for chopping wood. You don't need one.

BUYING GEAR (717–721)

717. No one needs five rucksacks, but most of us, after a while, have a cupboard full of gear that is never used. Resell, repurpose, reuse.

718. If you visit an independent outdoor shop and ask for advice, take up the assistant's time and try stuff on, DO NOT then buy the item off the web. Buy it from the store that has devoted time and resources and trained people to you.

719. NEVER ask an independent to match the web price. This is how they make their living, put food on the table, buy from their own community, keep the wheels turning and the wolf from the door. Is £30 the price of your integrity?

A day pack for a walk in the South Pennines.

Look for a pack with loops to store walking poles when not in use.

GEAR (701–808)

720. Always follow the money with gear recommendations or reviews. If someone is saying that something is the best piece of kit and a must-have, ask why. Are they being paid to tell you about it? Or have they picked it because they thought it would be useful to them? If someone is telling you about the technical aspects of something, are they competent to do so? Are they experts either by qualification or experience? Social media is full of people telling you what is great. Make up your own mind, and don't be seduced by labels or personality. Companies who invest in people to endorse something do it to sell the product. There is nothing wrong in that. But always bear that in mind when you see someone telling you that a piece of gear is great.

721. Take a photograph of all your gear and the receipts for insurance purposes.

PACKS (722–749)

722. Walking rucksack, rucksack, pack – there seem to be so many ways of referring to it these days, and it comes in all shapes and sizes. For a walk around town, you might not even need a pack – a shoulder bag might do. But for walking outdoors, in the hills, you are going to need something different.

723. For day walks in lowland terrain where there are plenty of communities that can provide fuel and shelter and an easy(ish) escape home, a 25- to 30-litre day pack is generally more than sufficient. If you can't fit everything in for six to eight hours of walking, then you have probably packed too much.

724. Once you move from a few hours' lowland walking to higher ground, then the pack requirements might – should – change. Higher ground means longer days and more remote locations, so less human activity and a wider spread of weather systems. You need to be able to cater for all these, and that means carrying more kit and making things more robust. The packs you should be looking at, unless you are a fell runner or an ultralight aficionado, range from 35- to 55-litre capacity.

725. Upland and mountain packs come in two basic types: hillwalking and climbing, the difference being the amount of stuff hanging from the external surface. And the waist-belt support system.

726. The downside of climbing packs is that they are bereft of some niceties. There is no big hip belt with cushioned material that you can really tighten into the waist. No hip-belt pockets for those handy snacks and that phone. No side pockets for the drinks bottle. And no rain cover.

727. Hillwalking packs aren't designed for climbing up the vertical face of a mountain. They are designed to carry a load across varied, but essentially horizontal or moderately sloping, terrain.

728. Hillwalking packs are designed to help you keep going, spreading the load around your torso with cinch systems that can help you transfer the weight from shoulders to hips and back again without taking the pack off.

729. Look for a hillwalking pack with external side pockets to take a drinks bottle, rain covers stashed in the base, loops for poles and axes, and hydration pockets for bladders.

730. The back systems on walking packs can be complicated, with air gaps, ways to alter the length, internal frames of metal, plastic or wood, and acres of cushioning. Many have hip-belt pockets, including one for that all important phone.

GEAR (701–808)

731. Hillwalking packs are often gender-specific, which can dictate sizing in the width and length of the back systems, and the waist belts.

732. Always try a pack out in the shop by loading it with your standard contents. Try different packs.

733. Backpacks for use in long-distance walking, camping and multiple days out on the hill start at the 50-litre size and go up to around 80-litre capacity. Once you stray into this terrain, you need to seriously think about your needs.

734. A backpack needs to carry weight comfortably over several days. It needs to be able to pack all your required items in and keep them safe and dry. Pick a trekking pack that has a weight-distribution system that you can alter on the fly and that will give those shoulders and hips a much-needed rest.

735. A backpack should fit snugly into your human frame so that it doesn't swing around wildly, knocking you off the trail. It should be able to hold items on the outside like foam mats, drinks bottles, poles and axes.

736. Don't load the exterior up with the contents of your kitchen – it will cantilever the weight off your back, causing untold damage and making one hell of a noise as you walk across the pristine silence of a moor. Try not to have any weight hanging off the back of the pack, but instead try to keep weight pulling straight down the line of the pack, so that you can keep the centre of gravity as close to your body as possible. This will ease walking.

737. Get a backpack that has a separate compartment on the bottom for wet things or a tent. This keeps the moisture away from the other items. A pack that has a side opening and a front opening as well as the normal top-loading access allows you to get at things without disturbing the whole pack. An extendable lid is great for holding that sleeping mat or just increasing the capacity of the pack.

738. Develop a packing system for the rucksack so that you know where every item is and can find it easily in a storm or in the dark.

739. Loading any pack is an art well worth spending time on. The aim is to keep the weight as close to your centre of gravity as possible (*tip 736*) while maintaining a system that provides access to everything. Store soft, little-used items in the bottom. A bivvy tent is good for making a soft base and it protects more vulnerable items. On top of this, place the first aid kit, emergency rations, spare gear like compass, batteries, sewing kit, laces and all the items that you will probably never use but will need as soon as you remove them. Then place your extra layer – down jacket, fleece, whatever it is – along with the waterproof trousers, on top of that. The next layer is the food and/or cooking system, camera gear and finally the outer rain shell. In the lid, I keep a head torch, hat, gloves, toilet paper and bags, and water filter. In the hydration pocket, I have a bladder, spare map and sit mat. In the pack's side pockets, I have water bottles. On the front of the pack, my poles. In the hip pockets, I have some snacks for both me and Scout and some dog bags should Scout get a call of nature.

740. I carry a OMM Trio chest pack, which holds pencil, notebook, map, compass and treats. These are the things I will access on a regular basis throughout the day. The chest pack is attached to my sternum strap on the pack by two small carabiners, so that it is secure and can be easily removed when I stop.

741. I use dry sacks of different colours to keep items clean and separated. This makes getting something out of the pack a lot easier. The green dry sack contains the first aid. The black, spare gloves and hats. The orange, camera gear. The blue, food.

742. I also use a large liner as the first line of defence. Rucksacks are not waterproof and aren't designed to be – that's why they have rain covers. But a liner adds an extra layer of protection at very little cost in weight. It allows me to store items of clothing such as my belay jacket without using a dry sack. This means I can stuff it into every nook and cranny, filling up the space and adding security to the other more fragile items.

743. My bivvy bag and Therm-a-Rest sleeping mat get folded flat and packed down the back of the pack on the inside. This frees up space and adds a degree of protection to the air mat.

744. To fill in space and add cushioning, I stuff my synthetic thermal jacket into the crevices.

745. Work on the gear in your pack. If you have not used an item for several walks, do you really need it in the pack, or could you save weight by leaving it at home? Refer to the basic list.

746. Use dry bags – either one big one or several smaller ones – to keep electronic items safe and dry.

747. When packing a rucksack, put your water bottle below or away from expensive electrical gear in case of leaks.

748. If they don't already have them, fit short loops of paracord to the zips to make them easier to operate in wet and cold weather when you have gloves on. Make one or two of the paracord loops luminescent with a spot of enamel paint so that you can see the pack in the darkness.

749. Always check the ground before you put your pack down. A friend dropped his off one night only to find he had placed it on the top of a massive human dump. He walked downwind of us the rest of the way.

HEAD TORCHES (750–759)

750. If you are walking at night, have a small red light fixed to your pack.

751. Head torches light the way ahead. Hand torches can light the ground immediately at your feet.

752. Use a head torch that has a rechargeable battery and buy a second battery as a spare. It will save you in the long run. Keep the head torch and spare battery in a dry bag, stored in the rucksack lid.

753. Make things dual purpose with a backup option. If you have a rechargeable head torch, make sure it also takes standard batteries as a backup.

754. Disconnect your torch battery when not in use to stop it accidentally switching on.

755. If you have a reactive head torch, where the beam adjusts to how far it needs to travel, think about turning the reactive system off. In fog or mist, the torch will struggle to stay focused as the sensor will be constantly trying to adjust the beam because of the reflection from the atmosphere around you.

756. Only use your torch at night when you have to. Allow your eyes to become used to the fading light. On a full-moon night, you might not even need a torch.

757. If you are in a group, turn your light off when talking to someone so that you don't destroy their night vision.

758. Make sure the head torch is helmet-compatible if you intend to go scrambling or winter walking.

759. Head torches just don't work with a peaked cap.

WALKING POLES (760–766)

760. Walking poles reduce the amount of force placed on your joints, especially knees. Use walking poles whenever you feel they are necessary. That might be all the time. When they are not in use, store them in the proper places on your pack. Never walk with them pointing away from you, to save stabbing a fellow walker.

761. Use poles to support ascents and descents and walking across rough terrain. Adjustable-length poles enable you to walk more easily across slopes. Reduce the length on the up-slope pole and do the opposite on the down-slope pole to maintain balance.

762. Zed poles are more compact and useful for travelling but have a limited range of length adjustment. Clipped poles are longer but can be adjusted to any length.

763. Make sure you keep everything lubricated and clean on any type of pole. Zed poles are prone to sticking on the handle slide, as is the little button that locks the handle in position. Make sure these are well maintained.

764. Clipped poles can begin to slide after some use. This is because the locking mechanism has loosened and the nut at the back of the clip just needs tightening up again. Do this when the pole is in its walking position, the length that you want to use it. Click the lock and tighten the nut so that it has a firm resistance when you unlock it and lock it again.

765. The strap on a walking pole is not just for hanging the thing off your arm when going over a stile. Its main function is to support the wrist and absorb the force of the pole as it hits the ground.

766. Walking poles have two types of basket: small for a standard walk, and wide for winter so that the poles will not keep sinking into the snow.

COOKING (767–780)

767. Take a stove and know how to work it. Jetboil stoves are great but take up room. Pocket rockets such as the MSR stoves are compact but need cooking pots. A small stove can provide a hot drink and a hot meal and make a walk so much more enjoyable and exciting.

768. If you are using gas canisters, buy good quality ones. The gas will last longer and have a better burn. Experiment with the gas canister to learn how long it will last. Weigh the canister when new, then after each use until empty.

769. Try to use the same type of canister all the time – that way you will know instinctively how much gas is in it when you pick it up.

770. Always keep the plastic top on the canister to prevent accidental activation. Walking along while your pack quietly fills with gas is not conducive to a nice brew when you stop.

771. Always use the base stand of a stove to keep it balanced.

772. Keep animals away from stoves to prevent them getting burnt.

773. Use a windshield to speed up the cooking process by keeping heat close to the pan.

774. A flint and steel are the best way to light a stove. Take matches and a cheap BIC lighter as well. But the flint and steel are primary. The piezo lighters on stoves don't last two minutes, so don't rely on one.

775. If you are cooking in a tent, keep it well ventilated to prevent the gas emissions collecting and condensation building up. Use the vestibule. Think about having a stove that you can hang from a tent roof to save space on the floor.

776. Heat water up for a brew with the teabag in it. It makes a better brew and is much quicker.

777. Use ziplock bags for teabags, sachets of coffee, sugar, salt and pepper. Takeaway establishments seem to have good supplies of sugar, salt and pepper!

778. Use milk powder on longer walks, but for day walks take a small Nalgene bottle filled with fresh milk for a better brew.

779. A simple packable utensil is all that is needed. Use a longer spoon to enable you to stir things cooking in a bag.

780. Use a small Nalgene bottle for oil to cook with. Keep it away from everything else in its own bag.

Adjust the length of poles to walk safely on slopes. © *Alison Counsell*

Take care when descending steep sections. © *John Coefield*

Clean your boots regularly to keep the water out.

008

CLOTHING (809–918)

'Gear is expensive, so make good use of it.'

CLOTHING (809–918)

BASICS (809–822)

809. Walking clothing is a thing of personal choice. What works for one person may not work for another. This is fine if walking about town, or even on a short countryside walk. But once we begin to walk all day, away from civilisation, in terrain that becomes more and more remote as our walking experience develops, there are certain aspects of clothing that we do need to consider, enabling us to maintain a comfortable and safe personal environment.

810. The three-layer system works well for many people, but not all. A base layer takes moisture away from the skin, a mid-layer provides warmth, and an outer layer protects against the weather.

811. A single layer system, like the Buffalo, works directly against the skin and is superb in cold and inclement weather. The pile moves moisture from the skin surface and the outer shell keeps the rain out. No other item of clothing is needed.

812. For some body types, Gore-Tex works well as an outer layer; for others the directional system such as Páramo works better. No one system suits every walker. Membrane systems such as Gore-Tex use a thin sheet of technical fabric that allows water vapour created by a human body to escape through minute holes. Because raindrops are bigger than the vapour, rain cannot get through these same holes and so the body stays dry. Directional systems such as Páramo use a fabric layer that physically draws water vapour away from the body and passes it on to an intermediate layer that transports the water away, while an outer layer stops the wind and rain from getting in.

813. Work on your clothing system. Experiment and find out what works for you in different seasons.

814. One mistake most people make is being fixated on the idea that certain clothing can only be used in certain environments, so a lot of gear sits in cupboards waiting for its day of glory. There is no point spending £300 on a waterproof mountain jacket if it only gets used once or twice a year. Use it, constantly. You will get your money out of it and want less gear. Buy good quality gear, as in the long run it will save you money and that is the best excuse you can give yourself – or, more importantly, your partner – as to why you should buy it.

815. You will probably wear a different type of clothing for winter and summer. That is once you have got into all this walking activity and have started to want to perform as a seasoned walker. Up until then, you will probably keep going out in any rubbish and have just as good a time, but be just that bit wetter, colder and more uncomfortable, and some point think 'sod this for a lark' and head off to the nearest outdoor shop, credit card in hand.

816. If you buy some new piece of clothing, bring it into the house when everyone else is out. Stuff it in the back of the cupboard, wait a few weeks, then appear in it with the confidence that you have had it for ages and just never worn it. This doesn't work, but the illusion can stop you from having that immediate guilt trip after the shop assistant has given you the receipt.

817. Clean your gear as soon as you get home from a walk, particularly footwear. If the clothing has wetted out (become saturated through condensation), clean and re-proof it using the manufacturer's instructions.

818. Clean everything as per the manufacturer's instructions. It is that simple.

Find a layering system that works for you. © *Ian Bunting*

CLOTHING (809–918)

819. Keep gear clean. Clean kit works better, functions as it should, and is a mark of how good a person is at their job.

820. Wash the straps on wrist devices to stop that itch and rash from flaring up. Simple soap and water will do.

821. Clean boots and let them dry naturally. Old teacloths – ask your partner first (good tip, that's from experience) – are good at soaking up the moisture in boots.

822. Treat boots as per the manufacturer's instructions.

UNDERWEAR (823–829)

823. Underwear is the one item of clothing that tends to get forgotten about, until a long hike on a hot day when those cotton pants from that well-known high-street store are going to create havoc once they become active.

824. Cotton holds sweat so well. Holding moisture next to the skin creates friction and heat, and that begins the chafing process. Add to that some lovely sewing around the seams and edges that will swell and give a wonderful surface as rough as gritstone to wear away the top layer of skin and begin the process of blistering. The bum cheeks – well, the crack, really – is where all the action will take place, along with the crevices around the groin. Cotton pants can act like cheese-cutters between the bum cheeks. The flesh moving together and apart as we walk feeds the sweaty cotton ever deeper into the crack, and then starts to floss away at the most sensitive of areas. Cue the pulling away of trouser and pant, and the odd wide-legged walk, and the shooting off into bushes for a good scratch, which only makes things ten times worse.

825. Bras can also be a source of much discomfort and chafing, particularly with heavy packs that can press on the straps and underwiring. Think about wearing a technical sports bra, even taking in your loaded pack into the shop to see how they fit with each other.

826. When it comes to underwear, here are three really good tips that work.

827. Lose excess weight.

828. Use talcum around those sensitive bits.

829. Ditch the natural cheese-cutters. Wear technical fabric underwear that has room and no seams.

BASE LAYER (830–839)

830. Once away from those bits, the base layer is the foundation of the three-layer system. A base layer can help keep you warm in winter, and cool and dry in summer. Base layers come in two parts: above the hips and below the hips. They include leggings (which used to be called long johns, but that does not sound like something a hard mountain athlete would wear and would be bad for selling gear, so now they are called leggings). And a top, either full-sleeved or short-sleeved, with a crew or V-neck or zip neck.

831. Base-layer material can be a man-made technical fabric, or a natural fabric like merino wool.

832. Technical fabrics wick sweat away and keep the layer of air between the fabric and the body dry. This keeps the skin dry. They dry quickly. But they all begin to smell quite quickly too.

So many options: single layer Buffalo, directional Páramo and breathable membrane Gore-Tex.

833. Merino fabrics can be warmer and can hold a little more moisture close to the skin, but can also wick the sweat away more quickly. Their big advantage, other than a warm woolly layer next to the skin, is that they won't begin to smell for at least a few days. If you have one that does smell, the chances are it's not merino, but some hair from a shaggy dog that was cornered down the backstreets of Manchester.

834. Unless you are into those garments that are designed to keep pushing blood up the body and back to the heart, keep the base layer relatively free-fitting so that you don't feel trussed-up when walking.

835. The final layer next to the skin is the socks. Wear good socks, ones without seams that rub a blister in a mile or so. If need be, wear a liner sock too. These are great and act as a bearing, drawing heat and moisture away from the foot, keeping it dry and cool and free from blisters.

836. Liner socks are also good for people (just about all of us) who have different-sized feet. My left foot is slightly smaller than my right, so it slops around a little in boots. The solution is an extra liner sock, making three socks on the smaller foot, or a liner and a thicker outer sock. Who says socks have to look the same on each foot?

837. The sock is one area where a tight-fitting compression garment can work wonders for those steep uphills, as the compression keeps delivering fresh oxygenated blood to the leg muscles to power your way to the top. Compression socks do help on long and strenuous days.

838. Waterproof socks can be a big bonus on wet routes. If you are walking over rough moorland, expect boggy ground. After a few days, footwear can be sodden, and this is when waterproof socks come into their own.

839. In summer, the base layer applies only to the top half of the body, helping wick moisture away from the skin and out into the atmosphere. There should be no need for leggings in summer, even a British summer.

MID-LAYER (840–842)

840. Mid-layers can be any material. Fleece is common, or shirts made of technical fabrics. The purpose of the mid-layer is to transport moisture from the base layer to the outside, whether directly or via an outer layer. Mid-layers also help us keep warm in winter and act as windbreakers in warmer (but not warm) weather. Some are tight-fitting, some are loose – it is a personal preference. The only stipulation is that they work with the base layer in keeping you comfortable and safe.

Legwear needs to be made of strong material to protect you from dense vegetation. © *Alison Counsell*

841. Having a mid-layer like a full-button shirt gives good options when walking. Completely undone, the shirt can help vent heat away from the skin, keeping the body cool. Added to a base layer, the shirt can provide enough cover to keep you warm on a cool or windy day without having to resort to a heavy waterproof coat.

842. In harsh winters, a mid-layer such as the Rab VapourRise placed over a technical base layer can be sufficient when creating heat through exertion. The full-zip front can be opened to vent heat and closed when the chill hits. Combined with a waterproof outer layer, it can provide excellent protection when movement lessens and the body begins to cool.

LEGWEAR (843–847)

843. The legwear market has really grown in recent years. Maybe it is because the manufacturers have reached saturation point with the waterproof jacket, the base layer is now well and truly fixed, the mid-layer has been done to death, and there are only so many fleeces that can be marketed, so they have turned to what we wear on our legs.

844. You can walk in shorts in summer. Just don't walk across a grouse moor, as your legs will get scratched to pieces. And watch for ticks. Remember those cotton pants (*tip 824*)? Well, they provide a perfect environment for ticks when you wear shorts.

845. Legwear should give you freedom of movement, keep you dry, and keep you warm in winter and cool in summer – which might mean two separate garments.

846. Belts are good for keeping trousers up, but braces can be better for some people. Braces don't cinch the waist and allow for a lot more freedom of movement.

847. Wetted-out, saturated trousers can pull the garments down, increasing the potential for a stumble. Always make sure gear is properly waterproofed. And that belts or braces are regularly adjusted.

OUTER LAYER (848–856)

848. The outer layer is for protection from the inclement elements: wind, rain, snow.

849. Outer layers come in two main types: soft shell and hard shell.

850. Soft shell, where the material is soft to the touch, moves easily and generally silently, and repels water, wind and snow. Soft shells are good for our temperate climate, in lowland and moorland terrain, and in mountain terrain on good days. They are not as waterproof as hard shells, but perform well in the right conditions.

851. Hard shell is just that: a hard sheet of man-made textile that covers one or two layers of highly technical material designed to get rid of the condensation created by our own body. Hard shells make a noise when you move, will resist extreme conditions and are generally bomb-proof. The more you pay, the more you get. Hard shells are almost exclusive to mountain environments and bad weather. Look at any mountaineer on a winter route and they will almost exclusively be wearing hard-shell outer layers.

852. Nothing is entirely waterproof, and most of the wetness inside your waterproofs comes from the body. Half the time I hear people complaining that the waterproof jacket they just spent a few hundred quid on leaks, it is more to do with them picking the wrong garment for the day or not knowing how to use hi-tech gear.

853. The waterproof outer shell is essentially a piece of plastic sheeting designed to keep the rain from wetting you through. And therein lies the problem.

854. Keeping rain out means keeping holes closed, and that traps heat in, which turns to vapour that can't get out. Gore-Tex say they solved this with their membrane system, a thin piece of hi-tech plastic with holes in. It requires a differential of both temperature and humidity between the inside and the outside of the garment to work. If that differential fails, and in the UK that is not unlikely, the water is going to stay inside the garment and get you wet. So venting is key – and that might just get you wet.

855. Heavy rain, or post-holing along kilometres of deep snow, will wet out any gear. When the outer shell trousers get wet, they begin to sag, the weight of water pulling the fabric down so that the seat starts to fall around your thighs and the ankle cuffs begin to bunch. This makes walking unpleasant and increasingly difficult, which can turn into a trip hazard (remember the accident chain in *tip 211*). Wearing braces can help keep the trousers from beginning to slip over the hips. From time to time, run your hands down the material, trapping it between your palms to squeeze water out of the textile and lessen the weight.

856. Avoid always folding your outer shells in the same way. This will create creases which become weak points in the material, eventually splitting. It is like folding a piece of paper repeatedly along the same crease. Screw the shells up randomly rather than having a nice neat fold your mother would be proud of.

JACKETS (857–878)

857. Walking jackets come in all shapes and sizes and for every conceivable reason. Always try one on before you buy. When you go to the shop, wear the clothes you will be wearing when you intend to use the jacket. This will help you assess how the jacket will feel and how much movement you will have.

858. Jackets are shaped, and this can be important. The most widely used shapes are the regular and the alpine. Regular is for a standard walking coat and is basically shaped like most people you see walking down the street. Alpine is shaped for rock climbers – generally thin, highly trained athletes who have that inverted-triangle figure I wish I had but will never attain, no matter what my wife says I could do if I put my mind to it. The inverted-triangle shape of an alpine jacket will play havoc with your waist if you are built for a regular shape. It might seem good to stride out wearing that ME Lhotse, but if you can't close the zip over your stomach (too many chippy teas) then it's a waste of a lot of money.

859. When looking at getting a jacket, make sure everything functions properly. Velcro is much used these days as a fastener, but make sure it works well and does not encroach on any areas of skin. Having something scratchy rubbing against raw skin is not a pleasant thing.

860. Zips are really important. You don't want the same sort as on your everyday clothes. They need to withstand the abuse of the outdoors. Is it easy to get at all the pocket zips? Move the zips up and down – every one. Do they catch in the closure material? If so, why? Do you need to pull a zip in a certain way, or does the closure catch whichever way you pull it? If the latter, discard the jacket. If it happens in the shop, it will happen on the hill, which is just annoying – and could lead to worse if a zip gets well and truly stuck and you can't stop the rain getting in.

861. In the shop – and the assistant might look at you oddly – close your eyes and put the coat on and operate all the zips. Do this with and without a rucksack. Try the hood: are the closure pull-strings easy to find and operate? Check that sensitive areas, like under the arms and around the neck, are free of any sharp ends of nylon thread. Closing your eyes is the same as being in the dark at night. Except you are in a shop with lots of people looking at you. It's your life, not theirs. Run your hand over the seams and feel for anything that will irritate. If you have any concerns, don't buy the item.

862. Storm flaps help keep the rain from soaking your clothes around the chest, which can be very uncomfortable. A high-end jacket will have storm flaps covering the main zip, pit zips and pocket zips, and may also have one running down the inside of the jacket closure. If the jacket does not have a storm flap at the front, check that the zip is waterproof. It probably isn't, but might be on expensive jackets.

863. Cinch straps around the wrist cuffs, whether Velcro or popper stud, are essential in a winter jacket. Pulling these tight will help keep your hands warm by warming the blood flowing up and down the wrists.

864. A waist cinch, despite looking a bit daft, can keep heat inside on epic storm days in the Cairngorms.

865. Jackets are a lot shorter these days, probably because the gear manufacturers want everyone to think they are alpinists in the Himalaya, when in fact most of us are slogging up a Lake District hill, or trying to get out of the rain hammering us on Kinder. Try to get a jacket that comes below the waist and covers your backside. This will help rain run off lower down your legs, keeping your underwear dry. There is nothing worse than feeling that first drizzle of cold rain working its way into your underpants.

866. Hoods are important. A hood should have adjustments all round, so that you can fit it exactly to the shape of your head.

867. Hoods provide a micro-climate around your face, holding warm air that is rising from your body and keeping the colder air outside at bay. Hoods are one of the easiest ways of quickly warming up on a cold, windy day.

868. Hoods can also help visibility in driving rain or snow. Make sure the hood has a wired peak that you can mould to your circumstances and also use to pull the hood forward to keep the rain out.

869. Practise walking with a hood to see how it affects your peripheral vision. It will. And that affects how you place your feet and hands, particularly on descents.

870. If you are scrambling or winter mountain walking, you might be wearing a helmet, so make sure the jacket is helmet-compatible.

871. A map pocket inside the coat can be useful, but in wet weather this means you will be unzipping your jacket and letting the rain and cold in. Find somewhere else to put your map, like the external map pocket in some waterproof over-trousers.

872. Use the map pocket in the jacket to store your phone. That way, if you have a tumble, the phone will be on you should you need to get help. Storing it here will also help keep it warm in winter, which will extend the life of the battery charge.

873. Make sure the back and shoulders of the jacket have extra protection, as these will take all the rubbing from the pack.

874. Make sure the hand pockets come below the waist belt of your pack. There is nothing worse than trying to extricate something quickly, only to find that you need to start undoing belts.

875. Always wash and care for your jacket as the manufacturer tells you. There is a reason for this. They know what works.

876. Rainwater should bead off a jacket, but after a period this will begin to diminish, and the fabric will need to have a DWR (durable water repellent) coating reapplied. If the jacket wets out, then it's time to wash and apply.

877. Try not to wear dark clothing on the hill. If you fall, it is much easier to see a bright colour than something the colour of rock. Have something reflective on your garments that will catch a beam of light as it sweeps around.

878. Beware of sharp, scratchy Velcro. It irritates, catches, and collects plant material and wool.

INSULATION (879–883)

879. A lightweight wind-stopper jacket can save you from getting too cold in windy conditions.

880. An insulation jacket will have down or synthetic fibre fill. Down is warmer until it gets wet, then loses its insulating properties. Synthetic is cooler but will still work when wet. Many jackets are now treated with a DWR coating to deal with light showers.

881. Put an insulated jacket that packs down small at the top of your pack. When you stop, put it on before you do anything else. It will immediately add warmth.

882. If the weather is cold but fine and you want to dry out your shell, take it off. Put the insulated jacket on to keep you warm. Then turn the outer shell inside out, throw it over a bush or rock and let the wind dry the condensation.

883. Walking in an insulated jacket will warm you up quickly, so don't do it for long periods. This garment is not a walking jacket, no matter how many times you see it being used as such in promotional photos.

GAITERS (884–891)

884. Gaiters need to be made of a strong material.

885. Gaiters that can be undone from the bottom without having to remove them are invaluable for adjusting laces.

886. Gaiters can help keep feet warm by protecting the lower legs and warming the blood as it flows around the feet.

887. Wear gaiters beneath waterproof over-trousers. This stops the rain running down between the two items and filling your boots with cold water.

888. Make sure the buckles are placed on the outside of the boot so that you don't trip over them as you walk along.

889. Always make sure the boot strap is tightened to prevent it catching on something as you walk along. And always make sure the strap is not degrading and becoming a trip hazard. If it is, replace it.

890. Gaiters help you walk across water. They keep the water away from the inside of your boot. For a time.

891. Keep gaiters clean. Don't allow dirt to build up because this will hold water and remove the gaiters' efficiency.

Experiment with different lacing systems for a better fit.

FOOTWEAR (892–906)

892. Boots, shoes, trail shoes, approach shoes, running shoes – whatever it is you wear, make sure they fit.

893. Visit the boot store in the afternoon after a walk. Take the socks that you normally wear on walks to try on with new footwear. If you use a special foot insert, take this with you for the fitting. Explain to the shop assistant what you want the footwear for, so they can help you choose the right product.

894. Wear boots at home for a day or two to make sure they fit well. Don't go on a massively long walk with a new pair of boots. Wear them in gently.

895. Learn different lacing systems to get the perfect fit for your feet. Help prevent blisters on toes by feeding the lace through the eyelets to make a square box around the toe area.

896. I have never slipped in a river wearing boots with a Vibram sole.

897. Keep footwear clean and well treated with the appropriate products.

898. B1 boots can be used in any season and are very flexible. This can cause problems in slippery snow as the flexibility constantly undermines the foot placement. B1 boots can be used with a C1 crampon.

899. B2 boots are firmer and much more robust, with some extra warmth. The sole still has a little flexibility, making walking long distances over dry, ordinary terrain comfortable, but the boots can accept a good C1 or C2 crampon to aid in winter walking and have a firmer edge.

900. B3 boots have a firm sole and are heavy. These will give the most positive placement in snow/ice when combined with crampons, but are generally too heavy for walking and restricted to winter climbing.

901. The best combination I have found for winter walking in the mountains is a B2 boot fitted with a C2 crampon.

902. Crampons come in different types and sizes. For winter walking, you need crampons that can cope with soft snow and ice and have the ability to keep you upright on sloping terrain.

CLOTHING (809–918)

903. Spikes are a popular choice and are good in soft snow and moderate terrain – lowland walking, for instance. They will give enough purchase on flat or low-angle terrain.

904. Choose crampons that have ten or twelve points, with the front two points being horizontal.

905. Having a heel bail makes a crampon quicker to fit and gives a positive lock, holding it firmly on the boot.

906. Buy crampons with anti-balling plates that push the snow away from the crampon base beneath the foot. This stops you walking on ever higher snow.

REPAIR, REUSE, REPURPOSE (907–918)

907. Gear is expensive, so make good use of it.

908. Repair items of kit. A tear can be fixed – on the fly with duct tape, at home with a sewing kit, or at a shop that does repairs. A hole in a jacket or trousers is easily mended, even if it is Gore-Tex. Glove seams can be re-stitched. Shirts can be patched.

909. Seek out repair shops for outdoor gear and get to know them. Make sure the repair shop knows how to work with technical materials. Use Gore-Tex patches to repair torn clothing that has been caught on barbed wire, the scourge of the natural navigator.

910. Learn to sew. Teach yourself the best stitching techniques so that repairs are long-lasting.

911. If a snap closure on a rucksack breaks, replace it with a new one. To do this, snip the end off the webbing and remove the broken closure. Then re-thread a new one and either double over the webbing and sew with two rows of zigzag stitching or leave it loose. Melt the ends of webbing with a lighter to prevent the threads from unravelling.

912. A bubble in a compass has no effect on its accuracy. To get a bubble out, place the compass in a warm place – on a windowsill in the sun is good – to expand the liquid inside the bezel and force the air out.

913. Check out charity shops in outdoor locations – there is always kit waiting to be reused.

914. Repurpose items. You might be surprised how good at it you are.

915. Turn old jackets and waterproof over-trousers into dry bags, dog coats or dog duvets.

916. A small length of foam pipe lagging kept in the pack can save a pair of ripped trousers if you need to get over a barbed wire fence.

917. Slip sit mats down the inside back of the pack to act as extra padding when not in use.

918. Old carrier bags folded make excellent sit mats and take up little room.

Outdoor shops like Alpkit are now operating recycling schemes.

Take time to admire the view. © *walkhighlands*

Always keep dogs on leads around sheep.

EVERYTHING ELSE (919–1001)

'Having breakfast while watching the sun creep over the horizon at dawn is a magical thing to experience. Make sure you do it at least once a year.'

EVERYTHING ELSE (919–1001)

FOOD AND DRINK (919–954)

919. The basic energy source you need is slow-burn carbohydrates. Porridge in the morning is a firm favourite, as is the full breakfast fry-up. Food and water are not only a source of fuel for the muscles – they also help power the brain.

920. The trick with food is to make it high-energy but low-weight. Carbs and protein give four calories of energy for every gram of weight. Fat gives nine calories of energy for the same weight. Personal preference should also play a part. No use having the perfect balance if it tastes awful. This is supposed to be fun. Cooking a meal can be great when out on a walk. Even a tin of soup or ravioli will be warming and filling. A hot meal on a cold windy day can make a huge difference to the level of enjoyment. If using a stove, use a wind-shield to conserve fuel.

921. There are two types of food you need on the hill. Food that is nutritious and of high calorific value to give you energy. And food that tastes nice but is absolute rubbish to give you comfort. It is one of life's mysteries why food that is good for you never tastes as good as junk.

922. Small Nalgene bottles can hold oil, sauce, hand sanitiser, garlic powder and anything else. They take up little room and won't leak.

923. What you eat before and during a walk will affect how your body responds to the activity. Always take a small amount of Imodium with you.

924. Store food items towards the top of the pack, to ease access and save them from becoming damaged.

925. Keep a small amount of snacking food within easy reach, so that when you stop to look at the view you can upload some energy without removing your pack.

926. During a walk, nuts, dried fruit and dried slices of vegetables, salted, provide a mix of taste and textures, and can provide energy throughout the day. Try adding M&M's, Starburst, wine gums and Swedish Fish for an extra hit, especially when approaching that hill.

927. There is nothing wrong with taking sandwiches, soup or something easy to cook that you find tasty and comforting. Having something to look forward to at a food stop is part of making a walk enjoyable. Sandwiches remain the most popular, with cheese and tomato still in the lead. Use a sandwich box to keep them from getting flattened.

928. High-sugar energy supplements such as chews and bars are great for that big hill coming up or for a quick boost. Fill up as you begin the approach, so your body has time to absorb the fuel. But beware of the drop after the sugar rush. Use these sparingly, if at all.

929. Flapjack is good, tastes better than energy supplements and can be made at home.

930. Make sure you take on a little salt on a walk, especially on hot days. This can help to rebalance the body's systems.

931. In winter, eat little and often if out in the open. Use trail mixes to keep energy levels up.

Get those calories in to power your walking.

932. Have a secret treat that you can share – some special chocolate or bit of baking that you can hand around as a surprise. This gives such a warm feeling to a group walk. It literally is worth its weight in food.

933. Ziplock bags are great for a trail mix, or nuts and raisins, or jelly babies. Never share, though.

934. There will always be an apple in the bottom of your rucksack. That is where the sweet rotting smell was emanating from.

935. Orange peel, banana skins, apple cores and fruit of any kind can last for years outdoors and they are unsightly to see. Take all peel and uneaten items home. Use a small dog-poo bag to wrap the peel in, then slip it into a pack pocket, making sure it does not fall out along the way. Take litter home with you and leave no trace of your stop other than footprints.

936. Clean hands with sanitiser before eating, after all those gates, stiles and walls.

937. Meals that you cook in the bag, adding water, are great for multi-day walks and backpacking trips. They are lightweight, easy to prepare and come in a massive variety. The advantage of cook-in-the-bag trail food is that everything is warm at the same time and heat is retained longer than having separate items to cook.

938. Check the weight of the gas canister before you set off and take a new one along if necessary.

939. Having breakfast while watching the sun creep over the horizon at dawn is a magical thing to experience. Make sure you do it at least once a year.

940. In summer and when the land is dry, think about not having a meal or drink that needs heating. A small stove that topples over on to tinder-dry grass can cause a huge amount of destruction to land and wildlife.

941. Never use an open fire. Ever.

942. Don't use disposable BBQs on dry ground, benches or tables. In fact, don't use them at all. Don't even buy one.

943. Carry a small amount of food for your dog. It stops them from staring at you and drooling while they watch you eat. At least for a few minutes.

944. At the end of a walk, nothing beats a chippy tea and a sausage for the dog. Learn the closing times of any chip shops that are situated at the end of a walk. The crushing disappointment at arriving after they have closed is sure ground for an argument.

945. Ditto, but opening times. Rushing a group along the route to make sure you get to the chippy before it closes, only to find it is shut on a Thursday, and it's Thursday, is a sure-fire recipe for lots of glaring and mutterings from the back.

946. Intake of fluid is a critical element when out on the hill. Go without water and the effects are felt almost immediately. A dry mouth, irritability and urinating less are all signs that the body needs a refill. Do not delay in taking on fluid.

947. Lack of fluid will begin to impair the brain, making thought processes more difficult; a state of unconsciousness could also be brought on, along with low blood pressure. Lack of fluids is serious and needs urgent medical attention. Do not delay in seeking emergency help.

948. Water is one of the best energy drinks of all. It is easily available from home and can be carried in a wide variety of containers. It is easily digested and is quickly absorbed by the human body, replenishing cells and tissue to maintain equilibrium.

949. Water can be sourced from the environment, with natural springs and streams on almost every walk. Always try to use running water and check upstream for anything that might suggest it's best to find another place. Dead sheep in the stream are a favourite in upland areas.

950. Always filter or boil water that you collect outdoors, to destroy any nasties and remove a lot of the debris that comes from a natural feed.

951. In winter as in summer, it is just as important to carry water for a dog. The sources may be frozen over, and while dogs seem to like munching on snow it does not get enough liquid into them. And if they have been enjoying a long day post-holing through the drifts, they will need lots of fluid.

952. Emergency rations are just that. For emergencies. Leave them alone.

953. Carry emergency rations that you never touch. Usually, a Mars bar and a small bag of nuts. Change them regularly – they are almost always skulking at the bottom of the pack in a dry bag that has never been opened. Make sure the items have a very long use-by date. I mean years, as you will generally only see them when clearing out your pack every six months or so.

954. If someone in your walking party is diabetic, ask them what to do if they become ill and need a hit of sugar. Ask them where their emergency rations are.

DOGS (955–976)

955. Make sure dogs are chipped and have an ID disc in case they are ever lost.

956. A harness for a dog is much better than a collar to attach a lead to. It gives more control and can be used with the longer leads that fit around your waist, allowing the dog to walk ahead and leaving your hands free.

957. Extending dog leads are a trip hazard to you and other walkers. Use a fixed lead for a dog.

958. Put a small falconry bell on to the dog's collar so that you can always hear where the dog is. Put a small light on to the collar for night-time walking.

959. A red dog jacket makes the dog much easier to see in woodland and from a distance.

960. Recall is the best behaviour you can teach a dog. Make sure you have a bomb-proof process. Always reward dogs when they come straight back on command.

961. Make sure dogs get plenty of hydration. Direct them to small pools and streams, and always carry some water and a bowl for them in case the land is dry.

962. Walking in hot weather can be dangerous, especially for animals. You need to pay real attention to fluid intake. Carry water for dogs in the mountains, especially in summer when water may be scarce. Dogs can also wear cooling coats, but these need cool water to keep the evaporation system working.

963. Dogs can be fickle with water. I have carried water all day for Scout and yet he has flatly refused to drink any when offered … only then minutes later to slurp water up from some muddy pool with all sorts floating on the top. I still carry water for Scout, knowing full well that he will probably not have any. So whenever the opportunity occurs I encourage him to drink from natural sources.

964. Dogs love high verges and hedgerows in late summer when they are full of blackcurrant berries. Pay attention to where these appear for a canine treat each year.

965. Dog backpacks are great for dogs. They can carry their own food, but not yours, water and other items. Whatever you put in a dog pack, make sure that it can't be affected by water. Dogs tend to jump into water without asking. Soggy dog biscuits are not something you want to be fishing out of the pockets.

966. Keep dogs on leads around sheep, to stop the sheep and the farmer unnecessarily worrying what the dog may do. Even if your dog has total recall and is trained to be around stock, there is no sense in putting people and livestock under stress. Always have dogs on leads at lambing time. No exceptions.

967. Be careful with dogs when crossing fields full of cows, and sometimes horses and donkeys. Be prepared to let your dog off the lead if the livestock begins to take too much interest. But be aware of any nearby roads that the dog could run on to.

968. If you come to a field that has cows and you are not confident, ask the farmer if you can use adjacent fields free of livestock. If you need to enter another field to remain safe, do so. Even if it means climbing over a wall.

969. Give livestock a wide berth when crossing a field with a dog. Keep the dog on a short lead and stay quiet except for saying words of encouragement to the dog in a low voice. If cows begin to move towards you, head for a boundary that you can escape over if need be, but keep the pace steady, don't run and keep heading for the opposite end of the path. Never come between a calf and its mother, with or without a dog. If necessary, find another way across a field with a dog.

970. Never ever let your dog or encourage your dog to chase livestock or birds. The dog can be legally shot, and you could face prosecution and costs. Always keep yourself and your dog safe.

971. Keep dogs away from grouse seed trays, as the medicated grit might not be suitable for their digestive system.

972. Dogs may not be allowed on open access land, so check online before your walk. In the breeding season, keep dogs on a short lead.

973. When crossing a river with a dog, take the dog or your pack first, not both together.

974. Dogs' paws can ball up with snow, making walking uncomfortable for them. Keep checking on the pads and clear away any snow that has built up.

975. Think about snow boots for dogs who have paws that are susceptible to balling easily. If fitting boots to a dog, get them to practise walking in the house first. It will feel strange, but they will become used to them after just a few minutes. Try the boots with dog socks to prevent the paws becoming sore through abrasion.

976. If your dog becomes trapped on a crag or in a cave, dial 999 and ask for Police/Mountain Rescue. Never attempt to get to a cragfast or cavefast dog on your own. Wait for the rescue team to attend.

THE (UNOFFICIAL) LAWS OF WALKING (977–985)

977. Never forget 'Stiles Law'. Lost and found kit always balances out. For example, if you find a walking pole by a stile, you will lose a different walking pole by another stile later in the year.

978. A pound in the pocket is much lighter than a pound on the back.

979. You will pick up the wrong map.

980. A queue will form the moment you step towards the car park ticket machine.

981. As soon as you find a secluded spot to go to the toilet, a long line of walkers will walk past, each nodding in your direction and grinning.

982. When trying on clothing, leave optimism and self-image at home.

983. Never share food. Unless someone offers you some of theirs. Then share theirs but keep yours to yourself. This can lighten the load and get you used to walking on your own!

984. If you aren't carrying some form of chocolate, this book was wasted on you.

985. Never pick the packets that are on the bottom shelves in a shop. Scout once cost me £50 by peeing on a load of ready-made ginger sponge with caramel sauce. And that amount of pudding gets a bit much after a few helpings.

AND FINALLY ... (986–1001)

986. Put something back. Join a club, donate, help someone discover the hills.

987. Join a conservation group to help restore the countryside. Footpath maintenance, land clearance and tree-planting are all things we can do for future generations. Help count birds that are in danger of being wiped out from an area. It is a good way to get out and a good way to learn the habits of a particular species. Subscribe to local newsletters about the countryside and wildlife.

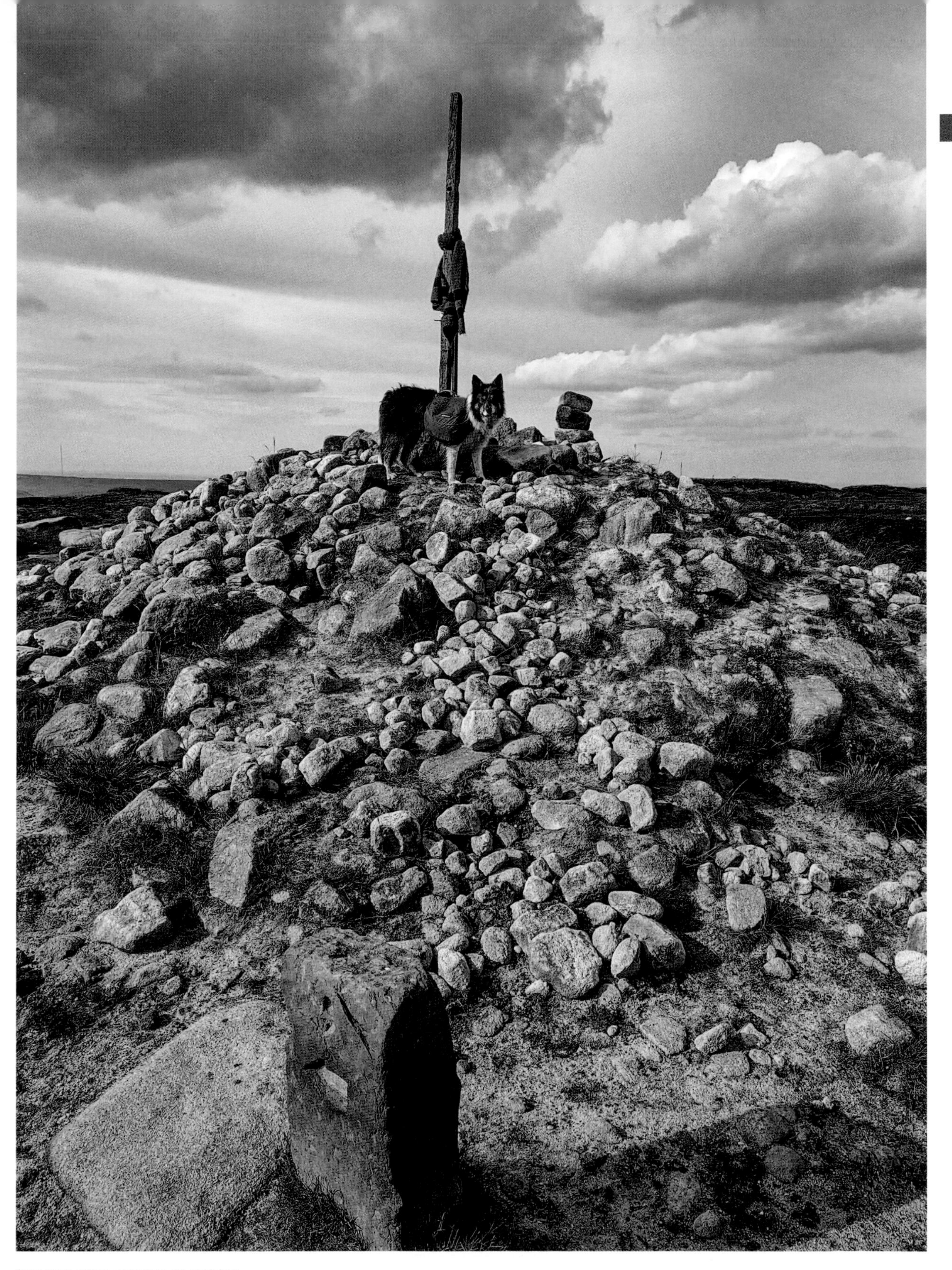

Spend lots of time outdoors with your dog.

Reconnect with the adventure of life.

EVERYTHING ELSE (919–1001)

988. Put some money in the Mountain Rescue collection tins. The teams are all funded by donations and need all the help they can get.

989. Become a supporter of Mountain Rescue and help raise funds and support operations.

990. Become a 'body' and help Mountain Rescue train to find people lost and injured on the hill. Especially brilliant when training with dogs.

991. Join Mountain Rescue or Lowland Rescue, the Ramblers, the British Mountaineering Council.

992. Donate unwanted kit to Gift Your Gear (***www.giftyourgear.com***), who can use it to help charities to get people outdoors.

993. Once a week, or a month, or a quarter, take a few bin bags and a litter picker and go and pick up rubbish somewhere, anywhere. Leave it somewhere for collection, informing the council or authority it needs collecting.
Don't tell anyone else.

994. Encourage children to take part in Duke of Edinburgh Award schemes to give them a taste for adventure.

995. Switch off the telly. Read instead. Immerse yourself in the literary environment.

996. Explore new experiences. Camp out in the back garden one night. Spend a night on the hill and go to work the next morning. Swim in a river. Leave the tent and use a bivvy. Learn to cook meals outdoors. Count stars. Watch double sunsets. At least once a year, walk somewhere new, try a new discipline, book the services of an expert. Place yourself outside your own daily world.

997. Keep a journal. All adventurers keep meticulous notes and collect items that have relevance. Do the same. Always have a notebook and pencil with you. Just jot down words that come to mind; note the weather, people, landscape, wildlife, feelings, anything that has a significance and plenty of things that, at the time, may not.

998. Invite your neighbours on a walk.

999. Bag Ordnance Survey triangulation pillars.

1000. The best walking companion is a dog.

1001. Be a record holder. Be the person who spends the most time outdoors. With your dog.

Enjoy the beauty of the natural world. © *walkhighlands*

The highest point in Yorkshire.

010

READING LIST

'A selection of books I've found useful.'

READING LIST

There are a huge number of books about walking. I've selected a few titles that you might find interesting and useful.

Hillwalking by Steve Long
Mountain Training UK, 2014.
ISBN: 9780954151195
The most authoritative book I have read on hillwalking. Whatever you need to know in more detail, it is probably here.

Navigation in the Mountains by Carlo Forte
Mountain Training UK, 2012.
ISBN: 9780954151157
There is something addictive about this book. You get to the point where you are so immersed in the subject of navigation that you forget about the landscape. Which is somewhat ironic.

International Mountain Trekking by Plas y Brenin instructional team
Mountain Training UK, 2013.
ISBN: 9780954151171
The best guide I know of for taking those first steps on the bigger days and weeks.

Winter Skills by Andy Cunningham and Allen Fyffe
Mountain Training UK, 2020.
ISBN: 9780993033711
Read this along with attending a course. It will provide a great foundation for the winter environment.

Mountaincraft and Leadership by Eric Langmuir
Mountain Leader Training Board, 2002.
ISBN: 9781850602956
The bible. OK, written well before the technology we have today, but the hillcraft is as relevant now as it was back then. If you get chance to grab a copy, and they are quite rare, do so.

Outdoor First Aid by Katherine Wills
Pesda Press, 2013.
ISBN: 9781906095352
I have personally never had to treat an injury in someone else while out walking on the hill. But I have had to treat myself and this book gave me the confidence to do so.

Invisible on Everest: Innovation and the Gear Makers by Mike Parsons and Mary Rose
Old City Publishing, 2002.
ISBN: 9780970414359
Mike founded Karrimor and then OMM, and what he doesn't know about gear isn't worth knowing.

Mastering Landscape Photography by David Taylor
Ammonite Press, 2014.
ISBN: 9781781450840
Lots of advice for those great shots.

Psychogeography by Merlin Coverley
Oldcastle Books, 2018.
ISBN: 9781842433478
Take your first steps into a totally different walking environment. Lots of ideas and thoughts to ponder.

The Natural Navigator by Tristan Gooley
Virgin Books, 2010.
ISBN: 9780753557983
I just love this book for how it connects me to the landscape and makes me think about the environment I am in.

GPS for Walkers by Clive Thomas
Crimson Publishing, 2001.
ISBN: 9780711744455
The best book I've read on using GPS devices.